Indian Take-Away: Offshore (Small to Medium-Sized Enterpris

Jim Downey

British Library Cataloguing-In-Publication Data

A Record of This Publication is available
from the British Library

ISBN 9781905363513

First Published September 2005 by Exposure Publishing
an imprint of Diggory Press and Meadow Books:
35 Stonefield Way, Burgess Hill, West Sussex, RH15 8DW,

Contents

Introduction

Media reporting of the offshore outsourcing ("offshoring") trend has reached fever pitch over the past few years with headlines such as "56,000 British jobs lost to India in just one year" and "New overseas call centres put our jobs at threat" in the British tabloid press. In the United States it has become a 'hot' political issue with politicians of all parties launching a fierce attack on American companies that use offshoring and numerous state governments making legislative moves to bar companies from federal contracts if they plan to move work abroad. Even in Continental Europe, isolated until recently from the extremes of the global outsourcing trend, politicians are alarmed by the number of companies threatening to move their manufacturing and service operations to lower cost environments such as India or Eastern Europe.

In response, many proponents of the trend (including consultants and big businesses) have produced mountains of statistics and reports demonstrating the economic benefits and competitive advantages of moving operations and processes to low-cost countries. They argue a protectionist approach harms competitiveness, future economic prosperity and jobs, while embracing the phenomenon can be a 'win-win' for both the offshore destination country and the country outsourcing the work, through increased productivity, better quality of services, faster product development and lower prices for consumers. They also claim it is easier for newspapers to print shock headlines about people's jobs going than it is to tell how, because of offshore outsourcing, companies in the West have remained highly competitive and continue to be some of the most influential and innovative in the world.

Throughout much of the last decade, small-to-medium sized enterprises (SMEs) have remained on the margins of this debate, tending to view offshore outsourcing as the preserve of larger businesses - the perception being that their smaller size and relative lack of business sophistication did not merit the effort involved in offshoring some of their activities. At the same time, SMEs were often unaware of the potential for their businesses and lacked the experience and access to resources needed to move operations overseas. However, there are signs that this situation is starting to change. This is being driven by a number of key factors:

1. Rapid improvements in technology and infrastructure have put the ability to globally network and outsource to remote locations in the hands of nearly every individual and business in the world and allowed operations to become more independent of location than ever before. Anyone with an Internet connection and entrepreneurial spirit can take advantage of offshoring, with relatively minimal effort. Even very small service providers and home-based consultants are now able to benefit from the growth of offshoring, by taking on numerous clients and projects and sub-contracting the work to an overseas provider in a lower-cost location – effectively managing the client and supplier relationship and outsourcing the rest.

2. The ability to recruit and retain local talent is becoming increasingly prohibitive, especially for many small businesses. The availability of high quality talent in developing markets, which is often scarce or deficient in the U.K. and U.S., is driving businesses to look abroad for their future labour requirements. In India alone, there are over two million English-speaking graduates coming onto the market each year (over a quarter of these are in computer-related subjects). While many of the jobs on offer may be perceived as unattractive by Western workers, in the developing world they are often seen as high prestige and can easily attract some of the best talent available.

3. Competitive and budgetary pressures, coupled with a shift in the balance of power towards customers (thanks in part to the Internet) have forced many companies to evaluate strategies to reduce costs in non-core processes and activities through offshore outsourcing while focusing their limited resources on core competencies and activities which drive consumer preference.

Whilst it is true to say that offshore outsourcing for SMEs is still in the early-adoption stage, there are many business owners who have already taken advantage of its huge potential. In the United States particularly, the trend is becoming widespread as domestic companies look to employ additional IT resource, back-office processing support and small-scale call centre facilities abroad. In an increasingly competitive age, offshoring is often a matter of survival for these businesses, especially where labour costs and overheads form a significant part of their total business expenditure.

There is still a great deal of hype (and hysteria) surrounding the issue, but at the same time no clear action plan coming out of the debate for many businesses. Most literature on the subject is aimed at large organisations and businesses with an existing global presence. This is a significant oversight, since the SME sector accounts for a substantial proportion of economic wealth in the developed world (40% of GDP in the U.K. is generated by some 3.7 million SMEs) and can benefit equally (if not more so) from the advantages of offshoring. At the same time, businesses in this sector face very different challenges from their larger counterparts. This book is written in an effort to help small-to-medium sized enterprises uncover the relevant strategic offshoring issues for their sector that have become so buried in all the media 'hype'.

Chapter 1

Offshoring – background to all the 'hype'

Offshoring has been variously described as the next business "must have", as "one of the most powerful tools a company has to improve bottom-line results" and as "part-and-parcel of doing business in the global economy". But some detractors have also described it as just another business 'fad', in the same way as the dot-com boom of the late 1990s. So why is there so much 'hype' around the subject at the moment and what is driving more and more companies across the globe to follow this trend?

Offshore outsourcing came about in the mid-1990s as a continuation of a long-term outsourcing trend towards relocating non-core activities in order to take advantage of global wage differences and the availability of skilled labour. Initially large, global corporations such as IBM, Microsoft, Hewlett Packard and GE Capital started the trend, attracted by the huge cost savings they could achieve by employing a skilled worker in India or The Philippines to do the same tasks as a Western employee, but at a fraction of the cost:

Country	IT Employee Cost*
China	£1,500 - £4,000 **
India	£2,500 - £6,000
Philippines	£3,000 - £4,000
Russia	£3,500 - £5,000 **
United Kingdom	£34,000 ****
United States	£40,000 ***

* [Source: NASSCOM, "The IT Industry of India" Feb 2004]
http://www.nasscom.org/artdisplay.asp?Art_id=2393
** [Source: neoIT, "Mapping Offshore Markets" Apr 2003]
http://www.neoit.com/pdfs/whitepapers/Mapping-Offshore-Markets.pdf
*** [Source: Economist, "Relocating the Back Office", Dec 2003]
**** [Source: PricewaterhouseCoopers U.K. Economic Outlook, March 2004]
Conversion £1 : $1.87

In addition to substantial cost savings, these businesses recognised that offshoring could help them:

- Offload non-core functions and free resources in their on-shore operations
- Avoid capital expenditure in non-core areas
- Improve business planning through greater flexibility of resources
- Improve their speed to market and service levels in core-product areas
- Gain access to specialist skills

They realised that offshoring could be a strategic move that goes well beyond tactical, short-term cost savings, to help them build sustainable competitive advantage.

However, it was after the dot-com crash in the early 21st Century when the practice became particularly popular. Many businesses (especially small IT businesses) were confronted with mounting cash-flow problems, as investors stayed away from high-tech companies which they felt were too risky. This was accompanied by a general economic slowdown that placed increasing budgetary pressures on many businesses to reduce costs, or go out of business. Faced with having to do more with less, these businesses began evaluating cheaper ways of working.

In California, for example, companies realised that in order to stay in business in Silicon Valley, they would need to use outsourcing – without it they simply couldn't survive. With the bursting of the dot-com bubble and fears of meltdown from the Year 2000 bug allayed, demand for immigrant IT workers in Silicon Valley and across the U.S. started to decline dramatically. Many Indian workers who had gained experience during this time began looking for ways of returning home to the sub-continent. This presented the U.S. technology industry and the returning workers with an opportunity. On the one hand, Indian technology workers had built up extensive knowledge, contacts and wealth during their time in the U.S. and could use this to set up their own businesses back in India, on the other U.S. companies were now desperate to find cheaper ways of accessing the same high quality skills, but at a lower cost.   Many companies set about actively supporting and funding new development centres in India that could provide them with ongoing resources, managed and controlled by former employees who knew their business and understood their needs. As a result of this dramatic change in circumstances, thousands of high-tech professionals in the U.S. (many of whom were new college graduates) were made redundant. Often these new graduates had studied IT degrees at university specifically because their job prospects seemed so strong just a few years before. In some cases they were even obliged by their employers to train an offshore replacement for their jobs, after which they were made redundant.

And so the offshoring industry entered a new, more vigorous stage in its development. What started with a small number of pioneering global businesses outsourcing a few support operations to offices in New Delhi and Mumbai was now being fuelled by a 'reverse-Diaspora' of returning IT workers to their homeland.   A new middle-class of Indian entrepreneur emerged that had the access to cheap labour in their back yard, financing and support from a network of clients in the U.S. and Europe and a worldwide business climate that demanded their lower-cost services in ever greater numbers.   This, coupled with advances in technology and communications, meant that the environment was almost ideal for expanding the concept of offshoring across the world and into newer and more valuable business sectors (business process outsourcing and call centres to name two).

Almost ideal, but not quite.   The global economic forces that sparked the offshoring phenomenon also fuelled an emotionally charged and highly politicised environment.   The backlash from displaced workers and the general fear that offshoring would cost people their jobs, eventually derailing their economy threatened to undermine momentum at a crucial stage.

Populist politicians have been quick to play on people's deep-seated concerns about offshoring and denounce it as an economic evil of our times (most famously John Kerry during his presidential election campaign in 2004 when he rounded on companies that offshore their operations by pronouncing that "all across America, companies have shut their doors, putting hardworking people out of a job, leaving entire communities without help or hope. We value an America that exports products, not jobs - and we believe American workers should never have to subsidize the loss of their own job"). The popular media across the developed world have readily joined in (and often led) the ensuing hysteria.

In the business world, some companies sought to gain virtue and publicity by pronouncing to the market that they would not use offshore labour, but continue to keep their operations in the domestic market. One leading U.K. trade union (Amicus) even bestowed a 'boss of the year' award on the CEO of insurance giant Legal & General for their decision to keep service delivery jobs in the U.K.

Political Capital – Keeping Your Business Onshore

A number of U.K. financial services groups have made it their policy not to move jobs abroad: Alliance & Leicester, Co-operative Bank, HBOS, Legal & General, Nationwide, Northern Rock, The Royal Bank of Scotland and Standard Life. According to Trevor Mathews, Chief Executive of Standard Life: "Some of our competitors have brutalised their customer service by taking costs out and transferring people to India. We have no plans to do that." However, there is little evidence to suggest that this strategy has so far reaped any great benefits in terms of increased revenues, or that the financial service companies that have pursued offshoring have suffered a mass exodus of disgruntled customers. On the contrary, some industry analysts will claim that it is the companies that have "offshored" some of their activities that are at the forefront of driving mortgage rates down in the U.K. and thereby increasing competition. The jury is still out on the political and financial capital that can be made by making a virtue of keeping things onshore.

A Matter of Free Trade

Many businesses see the offshoring phenomenon as a matter of economic survival in a globalised economy that is increasingly open to the forces of free trade.

As with the Internet, offshoring is not a 'fad' that will disappear over time. The principles that underpin the trend are rooted in fundamental business economics (i.e. the law of comparative advantage) and the values of free trade of goods and services. In 'The Wealth of Nations' written in 1776, Adam Smith demonstrated that by specialising in what they do best, workers in all countries would benefit. Even if one country is more efficient at producing goods and services than another, each would gain by specialising in what it does relatively better. Offshoring can be seen as a contemporary example of the law of comparative advantage.

Proponents of the free trade argument view it as a natural progression of global economics where ultimately everyone is a winner. What started with European colonisation in the 17th and 18th centuries and the "enforced trade" of slaves, spices and textiles has developed into the wholesale relocation of industries and jobs according to comparative advantages between economies. Where manufacturing industries have lead in the past, the service sector now follows, aided and abetted by the advances of the digital age.

A Win-Win Situation

To underline this argument, McKinsey & Company carried out a study in 2004 on offshore outsourcing and estimated that for every dollar a U.S. company spends abroad, between $1.45- $1.47 of value is created globally. Of this the U.S. captures $1.12- $1.14, while the receiving country captures on average 33 cents. The U.S. effectively captures 77% of the total value and generates a domestic return of 14%.

Their analysis of the offshoring benefits is split into four key areas: reduced costs, additional revenues, redeployed labour and repatriated earnings.

- Reduced costs for domestic firms – Offshoring generates savings that can be passed on to customers and investors. This benefits domestic customers in terms of greater purchasing power (through cheaper products) and businesses have higher profits (through savings) that can be reinvested into their operations. In turn, profitable businesses generate more jobs, contribute higher taxes and create wealth for investors that benefit the wider economy.

- Additional revenues – As revenues and incomes in the destination country increase, so does demand for Western products and services. This is particularly true for high-tech businesses. As Indian and Chinese technology firms grow, their demand for hardware, software and other products from the U.S. / Europe also grows – from Microsoft software packages and Dell computers, to Citibank banking services and VISA credit cards.

- Redeployed labour – With the transition of the global economy to a 'knowledge economy' or 'information society', the need for a highly skilled, educated labour force is stronger than ever. As some IT and lower-skilled service jobs go offshore, the developed economies are able to redeploy their labour force into jobs that create additional value to the economy. This enables businesses to focus on innovation and the creation of next generation goods and services that will grow their economies.

- Repatriated earnings – Many businesses that operate in the offshore arena are U.S. / European companies. They have established their own operations in India, China and other offshore locations and sell their services around the globe. The profits these businesses generate are repatriated to shareholders in their domestic markets and reinvested in the local economy.

It is important to keep job losses in perspective. It is true that America and Britain particularly have lost jobs to offshoring in the past few years, with the technology and financial services sectors taking the brunt of this. But job losses have not been as large as some politicians and media often suggest. America's unemployment rate in June 2005 was around 5.0 % (about average for the previous decade or so), whilst the U.K. rate was 4.7 %, the lowest in 20 years and one of the lowest in the developed world. Where job losses have occurred, the dynamic nature of these two economies has broadly been successful in reabsorbing displaced labour. Perhaps it is no coincidence. Both countries have been strong proponents of free trade over the years and both countries have experienced higher growth rates in the 1990s and early 21st Century than other developed, but more protectionist economies (e.g. the Eurozone countries).

Global Benefit

Furthermore, globalisation has proved to be a benefit to economies such as the U.K. and U.S.. Certainly the inflow of foreign direct investment (FDI) to the U.K. since 1990 has been a big factor in wealth creation and new employment. Today, over 40 % of U.K. GDP is created by inward investment (almost twice that of Germany) and there are now more new corporate headquarters being established in the U.K. than anywhere else in the world. As the CBI director general Digby Jones put it: "If ever a country was made for globalisation, it is Britain. It is in our DNA".

In the U.S., FDI accounts for only 12% of national wealth (GDP), but has been instrumental in creating new jobs across many industrial sectors. A study by the Information Technology Association of America (ITAA) in a report entitled "The Impact of Offshore IT Software and Services Outsourcing on the U.S. Economy and the IT Industry" estimates that by 2008, 200,000 U.S. jobs will have been lost to workers overseas, but more than 500,000 new jobs will be created in the U.S. as a result of offshoring. The Bureau of Labor Statistics (BLS) also estimates that four of the fastest growing ten industries and occupations will be in technology fields by 2012.

Alan Greenspan, Chairman of the Federal Reserve said in testimony before the Committee on Education and the Workforce in the U.S. House of Representatives [2004]: "History clearly shows, our economy is best served by full and vigorous engagement in the global economy... Time and again through our history, we have discovered that attempting to merely preserve the comfortable features of the present, rather than reaching for new levels of prosperity, is a sure path to stagnation." The fact is, it's easy to criticise globalisation, but behind many of the shock headlines about peoples jobs going, thousands more are being created by companies being able to compete and innovate better than ever before.

Consumer & Company Experience of Offshoring

Whilst the political argument for and against globalisation and offshoring has rumbled on, millions of consumers and businesses have had experience of offshoring first-hand – mainly through interaction with call centres and technical support services. However, their experiences have not always been favourable. Dell Computers were forced to bring some of their technical support back to the U.S. and Ireland after they received many complaints from customers who had difficulties communicating with support staff in India because of their heavy Indian accents. A number of businesses have also complained about low quality work produced by some Indian development teams. Others, who turned to offshoring to reduce cost, or who were obliged to do so by investors, reported communication difficulties and a high level of foreign labour attrition. This meant that they might request one thing, but end up with something completely different in return. They might work with one offshore worker for a couple of months and then suddenly find that person had left for another offshore operation meaning they had to re-brief a new worker on the project right from the beginning.

Some consumers have raised philosophical objections to their custom being given to workers in a foreign country (and therefore depriving local workers of jobs). Mindful of receiving bad publicity, this sentiment is often cited as one of the main reasons that companies defer plans to go offshore.

Interviews conducted by ICM Research in the U.K. with 1,008 adults [2004] uncovered some interesting perspectives from consumers on their experiences of offshore outsourcing. The research found:

- Most U.K. citizens are neutral towards offshoring to begin with and will give it a fair chance before forming a view. However, once they have had first-hand experience of offshore customer service, they tend to be much less positive about companies that offer it, indicating that their actual experience of using offshore services was negative.

- The main reasons for a lack of positive attitude was not so much based on a fear of poor customer service, but rather on worries about U.K. jobs and anger at the perceived greed of offshoring companies.

- Most of those who had dealt with an offshore contact centre considered the quality to be inferior to that given by a U.K. operation. Communication difficulties were the main issue, both in terms of accent and common cultural frames of reference. However, some of the U.K. public found offshore agents to be more friendly than their U.K. equivalents and quicker to answer the telephone.

- Relatively few customers are prepared to pay to speak with a U.K. agent – 63% say that they would never pay to keep the call onshore.

- Two-thirds of customers show a preference for speaking with a U.K. agent both for simple and complex enquiries. However, if the U.K. operation is closed, one-third of customers would prefer to call offshore immediately, rather than wait for the U.K. operation to re-open.

The summary of this research points to some interesting conclusions. Overall, customers in the U.K. have some considerable objections to offshoring based on a concern for job losses, a feeling that they are being 'short changed' by companies that offer it and practical issues around communication. However, when asked if they were willing to pay a premium for a service delivered locally, the majority of people responded that they were not. A Ventoro study in 2004 of 5,231 executives across North America and Europe supports this finding, noting that 92% of customers were willing to put aside their philosophical issues with offshore outsourcing in order to buy a lower cost product or service. Clearly, customers feel passionate about offshoring in principle, but their purchasing decisions indicate that cost is ultimately a more important consideration.

Customers today are far more discerning and demanding than before. They increasingly want choice in the way that they interface with service organisations and they want the convenience of being able to do so at a time that suits their busy lives. Recognising the difficulties companies face in providing such a wide choice of customer service on a 24/7 basis, the survey points to an underlying acceptance by customers that offshoring does allow greater flexibility and options for them to interact with their suppliers when they want.

The commercial implications for business of these findings demonstrate that there is still a long way to go in convincing the public of the benefits of offshoring. Indeed for companies that outsource customer-facing activities overseas (such as call centres and technical support services), the need to improve their PR on the subject is of critical importance – any cost saving benefits that are made from offshoring could easily be wiped-out by customer defection and lower sales if customers become disenchanted.

On the whole, however, companies' experience of offshoring has shown to be positive. Today over 40% of *Fortune*500 companies source their software services from Indian companies and a Confederation of British Industry (CBI) study in 2004 found that 30% of British businesses had outsourced some of their business activities abroad in recent years. Furthermore, a survey of 500 European companies by the United Nations Conference on Trade and Development, found that more than 80% of companies with experience of offshoring are satisfied with their results, reporting cost savings in the range of 20 - 40% with an average around 30%.

In addition, it appears that many of those companies that have already outsourced abroad are planning on increasing their offshore activities over the next few years. A poll by Chicago-based management consulting firm DiamondCluster International, found that 86% of U.S. companies plan to increase their use of offshore outsourcing in future – an indication that those who have experienced the offshoring phenomenon are becoming converts to it in greater numbers.

A Few Offshoring Myths

Often, when a new trend emerges or a change takes place, it is accompanied by uncertainty, misunderstanding and myth as those around it try to comprehend its impact on their lives. Offshoring is one area where common misconceptions abound. In the popular conscience there is a "cartoon version" of globalisation (according to Robert Reich, former U.S. Secretary of Labour), where people have created an image of work being sent to sweatshops in Asia for a pittance, fewer jobs at home and greater job and domestic insecurity. Whilst understandable, these myths are somewhat misguided:

1. <u>Work is sent to sweatshops for a pittance</u> – 'Sweatshop' is a hackneyed term. A job that pays less in another market does not make it a sweatshop. Unlike offshore manufacturing, which has in the past been found to violate basic safety standards, use child labour and exploit workers by failing to provide a living wage, the offshore service industry typically employs highly-skilled knowledge workers who have a good standard of education and who come from middle class backgrounds. These workers tend to be in the upper quartile of wage earners in those countries and the offices they work in are often state-of-the-art, modern facilities. As a result, the jobs are perceived as high prestige and can easily attract some of the best talent available.

2. <u>Offshoring means less onshore jobs for people in the U.S. / Europe</u> - Offshoring of jobs to India, China and elsewhere accounted for a small proportion of the 2.2 million jobs lost during 2001 - 2004 in the U.S. To attribute the majority of job losses to offshoring is misleading. Likewise, just a small proportion of the jobs that could go offshore actually will. According to a McKinsey Global Institute study in 2005, only 11% of service jobs could, even in theory, be performed remotely and many of them are unlikely to move offshore because managers are often reticent to manage operations thousands of miles away and burden themselves with extra travel. Many economists now argue that offshoring low value work to overseas locations will generate greater prosperity and more jobs for economies in the developed world by reducing prices and increasing labour productivity, which in turn drives a lower interest rate for the economy, an increase in investment and exports and the creation of more domestic employment.

3. <u>The infrastructure in offshore locations is poor</u> – The technology parks that have developed around the offshoring industry in places such as India, Malaysia, China and The Philippines are

some of the most advanced in the World. They have access to all the latest IT hardware and software innovations and provide back-up systems, satellite links and a support network of maintenance services. Having chosen to specialise in the provision of high-quality, low cost services these offshore locations can rival places such as Silicon Valley in terms of infrastructure.

4. Offshoring is risky and leads to a loss of control – There is an element of risk in moving operations overseas. However, advances in technology have significantly improved control of offshoring processes and Internet technology now means that companies of all sizes can access real time data on their operations thousands of miles away at the touch of a button. The risk of losing control through offshoring is often no greater than the risk from outsourcing to a local provider. Consultancy firms can also help to reduce risk by managing some of the transition and day-to-day management of the offshore service provider and avoiding some of the common pitfalls that can occur.

The Next Wave?

The next wave of offshore outsourcing effectively already started back in 2001 when the dot-com crash forced many small IT companies in Silicon Valley and across the United States to switch some of their development work to offshore providers in India. However, at this time the trend was still confined mainly to high-tech businesses based in the United States. What is now emerging is a much more noticeable upsurge in offshoring from smaller companies (some as small as five people) across the developed world, in industries as diverse as media, leisure, IT and financial services. They are moving not just IT development, but call centres and transaction processing to locations such as India, Pakistan, Malaysia, South Africa, The Philippines, Sri Lanka and China to leverage lower costs and improve service delivery.

However, at the same time another trend is emerging. Whilst much of the media focus in recent years has been trained on the loss of call centre jobs and data processing activities, there has been a growing migration of higher-skilled work, across multiple industries, which is causing a shift in the way offshoring is being used and perceived.

The E-Loan Experience

When E-Loan, a California based on-line lender, decided to look at offshoring they made a strategic decision to allow their home equity customers to choose whether they sent their work to India via outsourcing firm Wipro, or to keep the work in the U.S. If the work went to India it would take ten days lead-time to turnaround, if it stayed onshore it would take a further two days. Whilst this provided more choice to customers, it also increased complexity for E-Loan. They needed to have negotiated fully flexible contracts with Wipro to overcome the issues of minimum volume guarantees and termination clauses and be able to forecast the impact on their onshore team to ensure the right level of staffing in their U.S. offices.

Interestingly, about 85 percent of customers opted for the offshore option and the faster turnaround, but no customer asked for a cheaper price as a result. E-Loan may have overcome the political backlash surrounding offshoring by giving customers choice, but it remains to be seen if such an approach is sustainable. Eventually customers may be pushed further down the offshoring route if it means that there is an greater time or cost penalty to pay by choosing the onshore option.

Chapter 2

The Scope of Offshoring

Most offshoring is focused on clerical support, customer and supplier interaction, or internal support functions in relatively repetitive and low value activities. In the past three years, particularly, a number of companies have started to offshore higher value activities such as product and software development, financial analysis and business modelling. The distinction between core and non-core activities has become far more clearly defined and the scope of offshoring is expanding as a consequence.

While low value offshoring can be seen as an extension of traditional outsourcing (e.g. focused on lowest cost, highest efficiency), the offshoring of higher value work is a response to skills shortages in domestic markets and the availability of high quality talent in the developing markets. A study by the Corporate Executive Board in 2004 suggests that as much as 20% of offshoring in India in the previous three years was in 'high-end' strategic business activities. This shift heralds a new era for offshoring. It is becoming clear that offshoring has reached a new level of acceptability with business and executives increasingly willing to consider all areas as candidates for offshoring – there are no longer any 'sacred cows'.

Offshoring versus Outsourcing

The terms "outsourcing" and "offshoring" are often used synonymously but have different meanings. In essence, they distinguish between location and control of activities. For example, "offshoring" relates to the location where the work is performed rather than whether control of the process is in the hands of a third-party provider or in-house management. "Outsourcing", on the other hand, refers to the management of a specific process or project by a third-party regardless of location.

Outsourcing can be further categorised into the following three groups:

- Local – work is performed by a third-party provider in the company's own country.

- Near-shore – business processes are relocated to cheaper, but geographically closer locations. Major near-shoring destinations are Mexico and Canada for U.S. businesses, Ireland and Eastern Europe for European companies.

- Offshore – work is contracted out to overseas providers in locations that are geographically distant to the company's home country (e.g. India or Malaysia for North America / Europe).

Offshoring can be categorised as:

- Captive – where work is performed by an offshore operation that is owned (or majority owned) by the same company

- Third-party – the same as offshore outsourcing [above]

The decision-making processes behind offshoring and outsourcing are also separate. Companies that decide to outsource require a fundamental understanding of the processes and activities to be outsourced, the costs that drive those processes and activities, the capabilities of potential third-party providers and the risks involved in transferring control to them. Offshoring, on the other hand, requires a company to fully understand its own business objectives and the optimal location from which to source global resources to support these objectives.

Research by the McKinsey Global Institute (MGI) estimated that by 2001, 'local' outsourcing revenues (e.g. delivery of outsourced services in the domestic market) were worth in the region of $227 billion. As competitive pressure has grown companies have looked for even greater efficiencies and the tendency has been towards 'offshoring' activities to leverage even greater cost advantages. Offshoring to remote locations can be seen as a natural continuation and progression of the outsourcing trend.

By 2001, MGI estimated that the global offshoring market was worth over $32 billion. Since then, the market has grown exponentially and has become one of the fastest growing industries in the world. NASSCOM, the Indian 'National Association of Software and Service Companies', estimates that the export of IT software and services from India has grown by 40.2 % (CAGR) since 1998. If this growth rate continues, the offshoring market could be worth over $250 billion by 2008. The offshoring industry could soon become as big as outsourcing is now.

A further trend has emerged in the past few years, whereby companies are using a mixture of different sourcing options to deliver a project or service. This is colloquially known as 'right-sourcing' and has the benefit of allowing the client to choose the mix of resources that meet his / her specific requirements in terms of cost, quality, scale and timing. For example an offshore solution could form the whole of a development requirement or could be mixed with both outsourcing and in-house development to provide 24-hour coverage across numerous time-zones, or to take advantage of differing skill types. It can also have the advantage of spreading the project or service delivery risk across several delivery channels. However, risk is not always reduced and downsides are the need for additional project management resource to co-ordinate each delivery channel and facilitate effective communication and co-operation between participants. Without clearly defined roles and responsibilities the potential for conflict, duplication, lack of accountability and loss of control is huge.

One final expression that is currently used in the context of outsourcing is "home-shoring". This is effectively tele-working but with a new contemporary name and works on the principle that greater advances in technology and communications mean individual employees or contractors are now more able than ever to provide services to businesses from the comfort of their own homes. This avoids the need for business to make heavy investments in buildings and other overheads to support their activities. Whilst it is true that such working practices can achieve sizeable reductions in business overheads, it is unclear to what extent "home-shoring" can truly deliver cost and productivity benefits over offshoring or even outsourcing. The practicalities of managing, motivating and co-ordinating a disparate group of people and ensuring their compliance with business requirements and standards could outweigh the benefits of no longer requiring them to be physically located in the same place.

Offshoring Market – Room to Grow

According to a Booz Allen Hamilton report in September 2003, offshoring has been growing at double-digit rates in both the U.S. (11%) and Europe (12%) in the past few years and has expanded beyond IT help desks and HR services (e.g. payroll, employee record maintenance). Finance functions such as accounts payable, credit control and statutory reporting and even sophisticated IT services (e.g. IT applications development, systems analysis) are now being routinely delivered offshore.

For companies today, outsourcing is not simply about maximising efficiencies and reducing cost, but about creating value for their organisations. The key strategic question is "what is this company's purpose?" and therefore "how should the company be organised in order to achieve its objectives?" This is a significant shift from focusing exclusively on cost reduction.

Such a shift in thinking has been enabled by the growing availability of skills in parts of the developing world that meet (and sometimes exceed) the needs of businesses in more developed markets. In this context, cost considerations are only part of the equation – offshoring is a matter of accessing highly skilled knowledge workers that are in short supply or lacking in the necessary skills back home.

Increasing Strategic Use of Offshoring in the Organisation

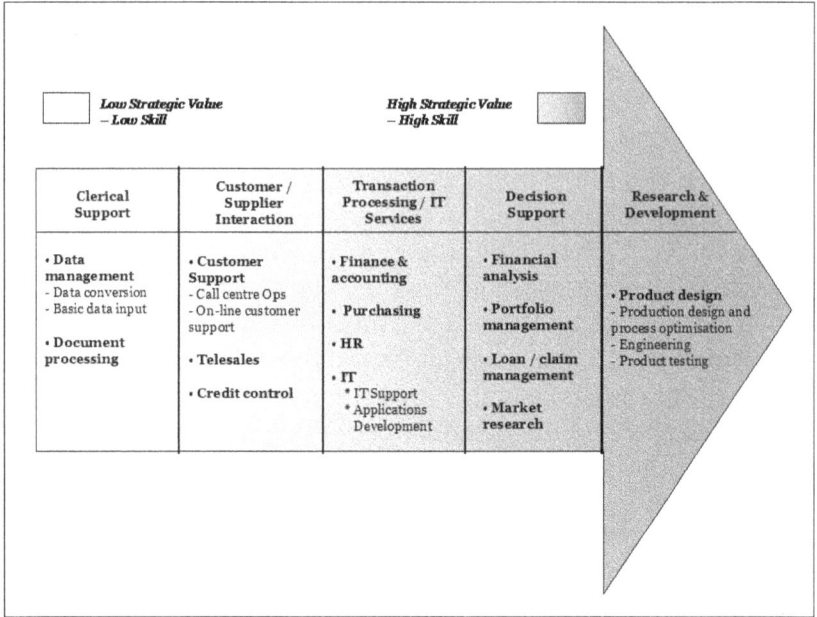

	Low Strategic Value – Low Skill		High Strategic Value – High Skill	
Clerical Support	**Customer / Supplier Interaction**	**Transaction Processing / IT Services**	**Decision Support**	**Research & Development**

• Data management
- Data conversion
- Basic data input
 	
• Document processing
	• Customer Support
	- Call centre Ops
	- On-line customer support
	
	• Telesales
	
	• Credit control
		• Finance & accounting
		
		• Purchasing
		
		• HR
		
		• IT
		  * IT Support
		  * Applications Development
			• Financial analysis
			
			• Portfolio management
			
			• Loan / claim management
			
			• Market research
				• Product design
				- Production design and process optimisation
				- Engineering
				- Product testing

The potential to offshore a whole range of more complex activities from decision support to research and development, is vast. According to some estimates of the offshore market, just 1% ($32 billion) of the $3 trillion worth of business operations that could be performed offshore have so far been moved *[Vivek Agrawal et. Al. "Offshoring and Beyond", McKinsey Quarterly 2003]*.

The financial services industry has been at the forefront of the offshoring trend in terms of process complexity – outsourcing a range of activities from general ledger accounting and payroll, to equity research, treasury management and even portfolio management. Specialist functions such as trust administration accounting are also being routinely outsourced abroad. Some banking institutions have gone even further. JPMorgan, Merrill Lynch, Lehman Brothers and Citicorp employ researchers in India to identify and translate financial information from company accounts around the world into international financial reporting standards for analysis. The U.S. banking, financial and insurance services industry is estimated to have saved $6 billion over the last four years by offshoring to India. As a result its costs have been between 7 – 10% lower than those of its European counterparts.

However, not every activity can be outsourced and not every activity that is outsourced will generate cost savings and productivity improvements. The key to success is in establishing a sound, compelling and realistic business case before embarking on any move.

Chapter 3

Offshoring – Not Just for the Big Boys

The SME sector is clearly a vital component in the growth engine of most developed economies. In the U.K., the SME sector generates 40% of U.K. GDP and employs over 12 million people and in the U.S. it employs over half of all private sector employees and was the largest creator of new jobs over the last decade (responsible for 73% of total job creation).

In the past, SMEs have tended to shy away from offshoring and outsourcing - seeing it as the preserve of larger corporations and of limited benefit to their size of business. It is true that in the past, the cost of communications and technology, coupled with the lack of suitable offshore service providers and advisory support have pushed offshoring beyond the reach of many smaller companies. However, there have been major changes in the offshoring landscape over the past few years that have opened up the possibilities of offshoring to businesses of any size and created new opportunities for small companies to make a step change in their performance.

The question is whether offshoring is really relevant to the SME sector and can provide solutions to the strategic issues that small businesses face? The answer is emphatically 'yes'.

Increased Competition for SMEs

Competition is not just limited to large companies. The same pricing pressures and increased consumer power that affects larger corporations, hits smaller businesses just as much - right through their value chain. Businesses of all sizes need to constantly find ways of making their cost base more competitive and minimise the resources consumed by lower value activities.

There is an economy-wide shift towards value that cuts across all industries, consumer segments, income groups and ages. Now, more than ever, consumers demand and expect to get better quality goods and services at lower prices. They are more aware of what is on offer and use the wealth of readily available information to identify and get the best of the best, the cheapest of cheapest and the newest of the new. Never before has so much information been accessible to so many people and never before have consumers been so far ahead of businesses in understanding the market and what is on offer. In fact, armed with all this information, consumers are increasingly confident and willing to try out previously unknown brands, in preference to established companies and products.

At the same time barriers to entry are falling for new entrepreneurs entering the market with low-cost business models and improved customer focus. The Internet is responsible for driving a lot of this new activity, allowing small players to challenge larger incumbents on a level playing field. However, the way consumers want to interact with goods and services have also changed over recent years. Consumers are no longer willing to accept mass media marketing and undifferentiated mass-market products. The new generation of consumers want products that match their specific needs and are customised to their lifestyles. They want a new and differentiated experience each time and they want it faster, easily available and at mass-market prices.

Small businesses are often well suited to meet these new consumer requirements. They tend to be more agile and flexible than larger, established companies and they are more geared-up to provide consumers with an individual experience which adds value to their products, rather than treating all consumers as stereotypes and giving them the same indifferent treatment every time.

This continuous shift in power towards the consumer has meant that the need to differentiate goods and services is more important than ever before. Consumers will pay a premium for products that deliver the quality they demand, but will no longer support additional costs for process and activities that add no additional value. This means that companies must continue to innovate, differentiate and engage with consumers, but at the same time reduce costs and focus on driving greater efficiencies.

Cost management is now a prerequisite for business survival. Any process or activity cost that does not directly contribute to improved consumer value or help establish consumer preference must be driven out of the business. Furthermore, this needs to be an ongoing, long-term process. Executives often treat cost reduction projects as ad-hoc initiatives to compensate for bad financial results or market setbacks. Enthusiasm often withers once a new project comes along or sales growth returns and the pressure on costs is no longer a focus. However, if companies are to survive long-term in the new age of consumer power, they need to embed a continuous cost management culture into their organisation and instigate sustainable initiatives that transform their business. Offshore outsourcing offers this transformation in a way that can fundamentally reshape the business model and company culture.

For small businesses, the demands for creating differentiation whilst reducing costs are disproportionately stronger than for larger players in the market. Large organisations are able to leverage economies of scale and synergies to cross-subsidise new initiatives and innovations. They can take a portfolio approach to creating new products - spreading the launch risk and development costs across a range of goods and services. Smaller companies have less scope to do this and have a greater need to fund new developments from cash flow earnings and borrowings. Smaller companies therefore have proportionally more to gain from offshoring than larger businesses.

Why SMEs Must Hire Abroad

In 1997, McKinsey & Company coined the term "the war for talent". In an increasingly digital age where knowledge and information are power, the need for highly-skilled talent is critical. The strength of a company's talent increasingly dictates success in the marketplace. However, at the same time it is becoming more difficult to attract and retain the right people, as demand for highly skilled people outstrips supply. With an ageing population in many developed economies and more people retiring early or 'down-shifting' for a better quality of life, the situation is only going to get worse.

SMEs are often at the back of the queue when it comes to their ability to attract high-calibre people – in general, they pay lower wages, offer less job security and provide fewer career development opportunities than larger firms. But without the right skills, companies can become trapped in a vicious circle of low skills / low wages / low productivity which in turn reduces their ability to innovate and attract investment in new technologies needed to drive their business forward. These businesses more than any, can benefit greatly from offshore outsourcing by accessing new skills and resources at significantly lower cost than they would be able to source locally. This in turn can lead to a virtuous circle of improved business performance, where competitive advantage is achieved through effective use of human resources and skills, improved return on capital and greater innovation. In addition, companies that have integrated offshore outsourcing into their business model are inevitably more attractive to venture capital firms, because they are likely to see a faster return on their investment. If a business has a faster 'time to market' and cheaper inputs as a result of offshoring, it will be more competitive.

Increasing 'red tape' and legislation is another factor which disproportionately affects smaller organisations over their larger counterparts. Employment protection and health and safety regulations can limit the size and growth of smaller companies where business owners perceive that the cost and management time required to comply with legislation outweighs the benefits of an increased workforce.

Managing staff is often the most time consuming activity for any business manager. Where this takes focus away from developing new business and managing relationships with customers and suppliers, business performance can suffer. Outsourcing can eliminate these issues by transfering staff management and regulatory compliance responsibilities to another operator. Often the offshore outsourcing provider will employ large numbers of staff, can improve HR costs and performance through economies of scale and best practice HR techniques and can afford the expertise to keep up to date with legislation. Where the offshore outsourcing provider is located in a less regulated market, the costs of compliance and restrictions on labour activity are likely to be lower still, creating further cost benefits and greater flexibility for the company outsourcing the work.

There is, of course, a moral debate which accompanies this approach as it brings into question the ethics of using weaker labour regulation for competitive advantage. In this respect, however, service sector businesses taking advantage of offshoring are no different from manufacturing sector businesses that shifted production to places such as China and Indonesia back in the 1970s and '80s. Using labour market flexibility to gain competitive advantage is nothing new and is something the U.K. government has often been accused of by its European counterparts through its use of 'opt-outs' and deregulation to attract foreign investment and jobs to the U.K. However, for the benefits of offshoring to be sustainable, it is important that companies in the West do not seek to exploit labour in developing markets, but rather ensure that working conditions are of a good standard in relation to the rest of the domestic labour market.

Flexibility & Scalability

Small firms are often more entrepreneurial and opportunistic than larger companies. Often operating in highly fragmented markets they need to seek opportunities and niches wherever they can. They are used to dealing with high degrees of uncertainty and tend to develop flexible structures to deal with new challenges and opportunities. In this context, offshore outsourcing fits well, especially where companies are open and receptive to new techniques. Outsourcing can give these companies the flexibility and scalability of resources to meet changes in demand and circumstances. It can also give them greater confidence to enter new markets and pursue new opportunities knowing that the risk of doing so has been mitigated somewhat by a lower cost structure elsewhere in the business.

The New Technology Landscape

It is only going to get easier for companies of all sizes to send business operations and functions overseas in future as the cost of technology and communications continues to fall. At the same time, there will be more offshore service providers who are geared up and ready to supply the SME market both in terms of their scale and the services they offer.

Over the past few years, large software providers (e.g. Oracle, SAP and Microsoft) have been coming under increased competitive pressure. For years these global conglomerates have tended to target large corporate businesses and generally enjoyed high revenues, access to significant capital and strong growth. However, strong competition in the corporate market, coupled with pressure from new entrants has pushed these large software companies towards targeting other areas of the market and launching sophisticated customised solutions for SMEs. Numerous well-known companies such as SAP, Hewlett Packard and Business Objects have committed significant resources to adapt their big-business systems applications to suit the needs of the SME market. The result is that many technologies and capabilities that were once only affordable for much larger organisations are now well within the reach of smaller firms.

At the same time, developments in Internet technology have allowed many of these solutions to be delivered directly to SMEs like never before. Through their Internet portals they can now access quick, easy and relatively inexpensive systems for customer relationship management, enterprise resource planning, human resource management and finance and accounting that can have a significant favourable impact on financial and operating performance. Thanks to the proliferation of new technologies, including cable, broadband and satellite and intense competition among providers, there are now few businesses that cannot access low-cost, high-speed Internet connections. This in turn has allowed small businesses to engage with suppliers, partners and customers much more freely by automating the transfer of data. Similarly, Internet links that are 'always on' allow employees to access applications remotely at any time and from any work station (including while they are on the move at airports, train stations, hotels, etc). No longer does a firm need to pay a licence for every desktop where an application is installed – it can now pay for software on a 'per use' basis where a charge is made for the amount of time a user connects with the software.

The advent of the Internet has created new opportunities for entrepreneurs across the world to take advantage of offshoring. By keying into a pool of skilled resources in countries with low average salaries, such as China, India or Bulgaria and using the Internet to link these resources together, they are now able to sell a wide variety of services to their domestic market, whilst taking advantage of the low-cost skills base.

E-commerce sites such as www.elance.com and www.rentacoder.com, have created active marketplaces for companies to offer their software development projects to foreign freelancers at rates that are extremely attractive by Western standards. These websites have developed sophisticated mechanisms for auctioning job requirements, documenting performance feedback and payment systems to protect participants from fraud. This type of Internet-based operation (a sort of eBay for offshore outsourcing) has opened offshoring up to SMEs in a significant way and created new ways for them to compete against their larger counterparts. Where large corporations have set up their own offshore operations in the past to access cheaper skills, small businesses can now access individual freelancers and offshore providers to create their own offshore network through the Internet.

With lower costs and barriers to entry, more companies will join the ranks of offshore outsourcers in India, Pakistan, China and across the developing world. Indeed, governments in these countries are so keen for their citizens to participate in the growth of global offshore services that they are heavily investing in political, legislative and structural support for the industry. This in turn is creating a new wave of offshoring destinations for potential outsourcing companies to choose from. Most of the offshoring activity in the past decade has been focused on the media-tech Indian cities of Bangalore, Mumbai and New Delhi. Soon even small towns and villages in India and across the globe will be able to offer services to businesses anywhere in the world. The advent of the Internet has enabled individuals and small businesses to contract freelancers from all over the world to get projects done at a minimum cost. The digital age is upon us and the opportunities for all are immense.

Chapter 4

The Impact of Offshoring on SME Growth

There are a number of stages in the growth of small businesses where outsourcing and offshoring specifically, can transform business performance. This can be through:

- Providing additional resources
- Creating the operational flexibility to respond more effectively to changes in market circumstances
- Driving down cost to improve cash-flow
- Handling staff management and overcoming cumbersome red tape and legislation
- Providing access to specialist skills

- As a business develops and grows, it must change the way it operates in order to survive. At each stage of development, outsourcing (and offshore outsourcing in particular) can play a key part in helping managers to minimise disruption, smooth the process of change and accelerate movement into the next phase.

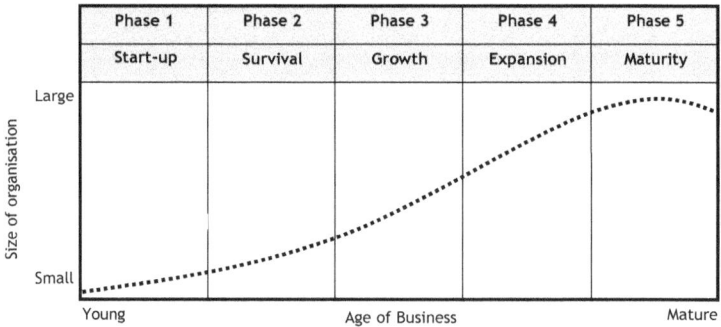

Phase 1	Phase 2	Phase 3	Phase 4	Phase 5
Start-up	Survival	Growth	Expansion	Maturity

Size of organisation: Large / Small
Age of Business: Young / Mature

Phase 1 – Start-up

The stimulus for starting a new business can be varied. According to the Annual Small Business Survey [2003] carried out by the U.K. Department of Trade & Industry (DTi):

- 29% of new business managers stated the wish to be independent and their own boss as the main rationale
- 14.5% cited a wish to make money
- 11.5% wanted to improve their careers and prospects

Whilst the catalyst for starting a new business may vary, the characteristics of start-up operations tend to be fairly similar:

- Initial growth is by innovation (i.e. the creation of a new product or service offering)
- Initial working capital is provided by the founder
- The core skill of the business is that of the founder (e.g. an engineer will often concentrate on product design and production rather than sales and marketing)
- Limited resources and an appreciation that the business may not be able to do everything itself

Often the start-up entrepreneur can be so focused on developing products and services and obtaining customers that many of the other skills required for successful business growth (especially finance and administration) are neglected. The founder's time, energy and money are rapidly consumed in meeting the priorities of production and customers. But equally important, if the business is to survive, is the need to generate positive cash flow and sustainable profitability. This in itself creates additional demands on the founder, who must adopt a new approach in order to manage different elements of the business.

It is in this context that offshoring can have such a powerful influence on business creation, development and success. By integrating offshore service delivery into the business model, start-ups can reduce their operating costs, reduce their need to invest up-front in technology (therefore reducing their working capital), gain access to specialist skills and increase their flexibility to respond to rapid growth in market demand. They can also gain advantages over their competitors through greater speed-to-market and faster returns on sales through a lower cost structure. The most popular activities for start-up operations to outsource tend to be systems development (e.g. design and maintenance of an e-business website or a new order management system), accounting and finance (provision of book-keeping and general accounting services) and sales and marketing (telemarketing, customer contact for order taking and customer support etc).

The downsides to outsourcing at the start-up stage can be the significant time required to set up an outsourcing arrangement (i.e. identifying appropriate offshore providers, agreeing requirements, negotiating terms, running trials and managing the relationship), the lack of knowledge of exactly what service is required and the level of demand for the service. One way around this is to work through an intermediary, such as an outsourcing consultant who manages much of the set-up and transition process on the company's behalf. The advantage to this is that it can avoid costly mistakes and improve the chances of project success. The disadvantage is that consultants can be costly and are often tied to a particular offshore service provider (and are therefore less impartial). The key is to find a consultant that can demonstrate relevant experience, provide objective advice and fit in well with the organisational culture. Where the company has already selected an offshore provider, there can be advantages of choosing a consultant who has a strong relationship with that provider, as this can help with the relationship management aspects of the project. An alternative is to outsource to a domestic company that uses offshore service providers themselves. This can save the start-up company considerable time and effort in supplier selection and management. The disadvantage of this approach, however, is that the cost savings are likely to be much lower than going to an offshore provider direct.

One of the key benefits of choosing to outsource at the initial start-up stage is that the business model for future growth is then established and ingrained in the company culture. It can become more complicated and disruptive to move to an outsourced business model at a later stage when processes, systems and staff are already in place and the business is focused on day-to-day operations. By choosing to defer the outsourcing decision to a later stage, companies risk having to deal with change management and business continuity issues (e.g. customer / supplier impact), while attempting to juggle long-term strategic projects and short-term business results.

Phase 2 – Survival

As a business expands from the initial stages of creation, the key issues become managing working capital, cash flow and the need for financing to support growth. Each of these issues drives complexity, the need for greater financial control and a large amount of business information.

Over-trading can often be an issue in the survival stage. Businesses are so focused on building a customer base and managing output that their uncontrolled growth precipitates cash-flow problems, customer service issues and loss of management control, which have the potential to bring a company down.

Outsourcing at this stage can serve to simplify business operations and help managers to focus on core business. It can also bring access to readily scalable resources for responding to sudden changes in business demand. By keeping outsourcing providers on a retainer basis, a business can maintain a pool of 'on-call' resources. The business benefits by knowing they can continue to pursue potential clients, whilst minimising the risk of over-trading. It also gives financial flexibility as fixed cost overheads are converted into variable costs that do not need to be supported by ongoing capital.

Phase 3 – Growth

By the time a business has entered the growth stage, it is likely to be operating profitably but may still be experiencing difficulties with cash flow. Demands on working capital are likely to remain high and most income is ploughed back into the business to support ongoing growth. There is often a 'glass ceiling' for businesses at this stage with a lack of funding, expertise and resources to move them into the next phase of development.

With growing business complexity, the business is likely to increase its staff recruitment and functional departments begin to appear. Often businesses begin to spend considerable time and effort managing human resources. This time and effort invested in people management can take significant focus away from core, value-creating activities of the business. Furthermore, a growing business will need to engage in research and development to expand their product portfolio and service offerings. Any new developments will require significant resources – time and money.

At this stage, offshore outsourcing offers several advantages:

- Eliminates the difficulties of recruiting, managing and retaining staff by moving human resource management to an external provider.
- Avoids the complexities of increasing employee regulation and legislation (which increase as the company grows in size) – especially if the provider is in a less regulated market.
- Removes non-core activities, freeing existing staff and management resource to focus on activities driving consumer preference and business growth.
- Complements on-shore, local resource during times of peak demand, or covers 24 hour working (i.e. 24-hour customer support) by leveraging the benefit of different time-zones

In addition, outsourcing can support the innovation and product development process by providing access to cutting-edge capabilities and techniques. With many offshore providers moving further up the value-chain, there are increasing opportunities for businesses to outsource much of the research and analysis stages of product development. Furthermore, if the outsourcer is involved early in the product development cycle, they will be better equipped to support the new product or service once it has been launched in the market.

Phase 4 – Expansion

As in the growth stage, a key issue during expansion is likely to be funding. Retained earnings are often still a critical element in supporting growth, but dividend payments are usually unavoidable in order to attract and retain investors and maintain the in-flow of capital. Along with the management of shareholder (and bank) expectations, comes the need for more sophisticated control systems, management information provision and formalised organisational structures.

Greater budgetary control, regular management reporting and increased internal controls are all fundamental to the effective operation of an organisation and the reduction of risk. However, they do little to add direct value to customers. They are a 'hygiene factor' and a burden that must be borne by the business without creating competitive advantage. An expanding business must minimise the cost of necessary non-value adding activities without increasing operational risk. Outsourcing offers the solution to these issues by providing services that integrate best-practice principles and greater efficiencies, with risk sharing, process improvements and leading edge technologies to drive down costs and improve business control.

With the 'formalising' of operations and greater shareholder scrutiny, businesses in this stage often go through what Larry Greiner, in his article for the *Harvard Business Review* (*entitled "Evolution and Revolution as Organisations Grow", July/August 1972*), describes as a "crisis of culture". As the business develops formal systems, procedures and policies and takes on 'professional' managers, the nature (or culture) of the business changes. People who have different motivations than the original founders of the business and who are less likely to make the same level of sacrifices, move in to run the business. Often this is what is required to take the business to the next level, but can be particularly uncomfortable for those involved in the business from its early stages. Outsourcing (and offshoring in particular) may be 'forced' on the company by its shareholders who are keen to drive down costs and maximise their returns. Often this type of offshoring is 'tactical' with a short-term cost focus. There is, however, a danger that internal management and staff may not be fully committed to support outsourcing if it is imposed on them and they see it as undermining their department / function / role in the organisation. They may also question the motives of the new owners / shareholders and managers if it is seen as a purely tactical move that simply delivers more cash to shareholders in the short-term rather than investing for future growth. In the past, outsourcing was often accompanied by asset stripping, where short-term investors sought to break up certain areas of an acquired business in order to sell them on for a higher return.

Potential outsourcers are unlikely to achieve sustainable benefits and cost savings they need if their focus is too short-term. This is because both sides of the outsourcing relationship are less likely to be committed to driving maximum business benefits than if the relationship is intended as a longer-term strategy. Outsourcing providers may also be less inclined to invest the technology, process improvements and people that drive lower costs if a contract is too short-term.

Strategic offshoring projects at this stage of a company's development can be invaluable in pushing the business to the next level. By putting in place an outsourced network of resources that offer consistent service, continuous improvement and investment in new technologies, companies can significantly enhance their operational capabilities and growth prospects.

Phase 5 – Maturity

Most businesses that reach this stage are in transition from small company to medium-large organisation. Although they are mature, they are likely to still be growing (albeit at a slower pace) and they will have well established operating procedures and a formalised structure. In addition, they are likely to be facing stronger competition from larger players and market consolidation of smaller players. Incumbent large companies will often employ their considerable economies of scale to attack on price in order to maintain market share. In response to increased competition a business may counter with lower prices, develop a new market opportunity, or direct resources to product and service quality improvements. All three tactics can involve considerable cost and will need to be supported elsewhere in the organisation with greater expense control and improved productivity.

Offshore outsourcing at this stage can be a strategic initiative to develop a new market opportunity (e.g. to provide new communication channels or develop new products and services cheaply), or simply as a means to long-term survival used to lower business costs and generate savings for investment in price reductions and marketing expenses.

Chapter 5

Getting Started

The key steps for any organisation looking at offshore outsourcing are:

1. Develop a robust, compelling business case
2. Engage internal support
3. Commit internal resources
4. Communicate progress to stakeholders

The Business Case

The business case is the first step to ensuring a sound foundation for the move. At this point the company needs to clarify its objectives, goals and scope for the project (i.e. cost savings, access to resources, etc) and determine whether offshore outsourcing will deliver these. Financial considerations are important and should include the full costs as well as the benefits of moving the activity offshore.

One of the key areas that the business case needs to address is what to outsource. There are certain activities that have been tried and tested overseas and have a good chance of working successfully for many new comers to the market. Examples of these are data-entry, transaction processing and simple reconciliations. The success rates for call centres and other voice processes tend to be more mixed. Incoming calls from existing customers are often the hardest to handle, because the service provision must be reactive, according to customer needs. Outbound calls to non-customers that follow a standard template are usually the least complex and least delicate and can be easier to move offshore. However, even the most straightforward activities can have underlying complexities. One example of this is reverification, where calls are made to potential borrowers to validate the information on their loan application forms. Because the calls are made to potential rather than existing customers, it's often hard to measure whether an operator has actually made the calls, or skipped some of them to save time. Because the cost of advancing a bad loan is so high, the risk of offshoring the reverification process could be very high. Of course there are solutions to this - quality checks, progress reports and call monitoring – but all of these activities add cost and need to be integrated into the business case and process design.

Experienced hands at offshoring may say that companies should only outsource their non-core activities, keeping core activities in-house. Broadly speaking this is a good rule of thumb. However, deciding what is core and non-core is not always so straightforward. Having a sound understanding of the company's strengths and weaknesses is a good starting point. Another approach is to ask "if I was starting the business again from scratch, would I choose to do this activity myself [i.e. rather than outsourcing it to someone else]?" and "do I do this activity so well that someone else would pay me to do it for them?" – if the answer to each of these questions is "no", the likelihood is that they are activities that would be better handled by someone else. Having a clear distinction between what is core and non-core is key to ensuring that the organisation's resources are focused on what it can do best. Without such clarity and a robust outsourcing strategy, the business may continue investing in non-core areas of the business to the detriment of core, strategic areas.

This is not to say that core business areas should never be outsourced. As companies experience the benefits of outsourcing, some have experimented by outsourcing areas that could be considered core to their businesses. Often this occurs once a business has built up experience in outsourcing non-core areas and feels confident that outsourcing works. It may also occur in response to a peak in workload in a core area, which requires additional support from outside the organisation. The key is for companies to feel comfortable with the business case for moving to an outsourcing provider (especially if the work is also being sent offshore), irrespective of what is to be moved.

Another common approach companies take is to move stand-alone functions offshore. However, companies should guard against simply offshoring mundane and tedious tasks. This is often a recipe for high labour attrition rates in the offshore operation, with consequent negative effects on both business performance and process costs.

Once the business case has established the rationale for outsourcing and costs and benefits have been identified, the final stage is to measure performance of the existing operation as a baseline and develop forecasts of the expected performance following the offshore move. This will help justify the business effort required to make the move and can enable targets to be set to measure whether the initiative is successful or not. It can also provide opportunities to improve the process or operation before sending it overseas.

Business Case Checklist

The following provides a checklist for companies developing an offshore business case:

- Processes which could be outsourced to achieve improvements in efficiency
- Stakeholder commitment and approval to outsourcing the processes in question
- Risks involved in moving operations overseas and how to mitigate them
- Who can and will provide the offshore services and their location
- Skills and capabilities required by the offshore service provider
- Service levels that are required to operate the services effectively
- Tax and legal requirements to be met in transferring operations
- How to transfer knowledge effectively to the offshore service provider
- How business continuity will be maintained throughout the transition
- Change management issues that need to be addressed
- How to measure success

Engage Internal Support

Developing a factual, objective business case for the offshoring decision is critical in achieving broad internal support. As with any business change initiative, support must exist at the top of the organisation and key stakeholders need to have the opportunity to engage with the decision-making process. The key to building support is to demonstrate the advantages for each key stakeholder group, whilst listening closely to any concerns they may express. It is also crucial to engage with other employee groups throughout the organisation to prevent the project from stalling through staff alienation or fear of change.

Commit Internal Resources

Once internal support has been secured, the next stage is to commit business resources to making the initiative happen. This will usually involve appointing a project team and manager with responsibility for fulfilling the project's objectives, goals and scope. A steering committee is also highly recommended to oversee the process and ensure that the company remains focused on executing the project successfully. An offshore outsourcing expert should be engaged on the project (either an internal resource who works with the core team as required, or a consultant who can be called upon to help manage the offshoring process and give advice).

It is important that where staff are not engaged full-time on the project, their existing responsibilities are carefully managed to ensure that sufficient time and focus can be given to the project. Likewise, full-time members will need to have their responsibilities fulfilled by additional resource elsewhere in the business and know that their future career in the organisation is assured once the project is complete.

The commitment of financial resources is also critical to the success of the project and should always include a contingency (a figure of 10-15% over the business case costing is recommended as a minimum). This should be handled by way of a budget which is owned and managed by the project manager and supervised by the steering committee.

Communication

Communicating progress is also key to ensuring that the project maintains internal support and allows for any issues to be identified and resolved quickly. Communication between core team members, the stakeholders they represent and any third-party providers needs to be continuous, to facilitate problem solving and management of the unexpected.

Ongoing communication of the project's success and the business benefits it brings is also a key component in ensuring that the business maintains an open attitude towards the initiative and remains receptive to any future developments.

Making the Move

For anyone contemplating outsourcing work to a location thousands of miles away, the first step is usually the most daunting. Once the business case has been established, the objectives, goals and scope have been clearly defined, internal support has been secured and the company is ready to go through the cultural and organisational changes required, they need to select the right offshore delivery model – build or buy.

With concerns running high about the security of offshore providers and the risk of fraud and intellectual property piracy, businesses are often tempted towards developing their own offshore facility. However, for SMEs this is less practical and in any case, may be unnecessary. Building an inhouse, offshore facility (known as a 'captive' operation) can be useful if a business already has experience of working in the offshore destination country and can successfully capacity-build a team with the right skills and experience. However, the cost implications also need to be considered and such a strategy should be pursued only if:

- The right offshore provider is not already available in the chosen destination country
- The cost of an offshore provider developing the required capability is uneconomical
- The business need is highly predictable

Furthermore, the business needs to be sure that it can and wants to commit to an offshore facility for a long-period, as a captive option tends to be more permanent.

Buying offshore resources is the most popular way of moving offshore and probably the best route for any SME. There are a number of reasons for this:

- <u>Cost</u> – managing remote teams is a costly business. Offshore providers tend to have established teams, ways of working and managerial structures that are cost-effective. Offshoring is their 'core' business and the economies of scale and process knowledge they have developed are likely to be difficult to beat.
- <u>Productivity</u> – offshore providers make their money by maximising their return on assets and optimising productivity. For a business to achieve this from scratch in a captive operation would probably take substantially more time than working with the offshore provider.
- <u>Added Value</u> – offshore providers constantly look for ways to move 'up the value chain' in order to sell more business. They are experts in their field and have often developed innovative solutions that could help clients significantly improve their business operations and improve productivity.
- <u>Flexibility</u> – offshore providers give ready access to a large pool of resources that can be called upon as market conditions change or new opportunities emerge. They can provide greater flexibility than captive operations by adapting quickly to changes in technology without having to bear the time and cost of retraining internal staff.

Another option is the Build-Operate-Transfer model. This is where an offshore provider builds an offshore operation on the customer's behalf, using their knowledge, experience and capabilities. Once the operation is up and running, the customer buys it from the provider at a pre-determined price. The advantage of this approach is that it is low risk. If business circumstances change, the company is not obliged to take up the purchase option. It may be a credible option for an SME, as long as they can negotiate effectively with the offshore provider and are able to monitor progress closely as the offshore operation develops. The disadvantage to this option is higher cost – with the offshore provider charging a premium in return for taking a greater risk.

Finally, there is the joint-venture approach which has been used with varying degrees of success in the financial services sector to drive cost savings and share risk, whilst maintaining an element of control and ownership. The downside to this approach is that it can result in a conflict of interest where one side seeks to maximise revenues and the other seeks to reduce costs.

Choosing the Right Offshore Provider

Today there are an estimated 10,000+ offshore service providers in over 175 different countries across the world (according to Ventoro, 2004). Clearly, with such a wide choice of supply options, it is critical that companies have robust processes for identifying and selecting the most appropriate offshore provider for their needs.

Traditionally, SMEs have tended to approach offshoring through intermediary providers such as consultants and agents. While many companies have found this to be a successful model (particularly if they have no prior experience of offshore outsourcing), the disadvantage is that they may lose some cost benefits. Intermediary providers earn a healthy margin on their costs. For companies that wish to engage intermediary providers over a long period of time, these margins can add up.

More recently, SMEs have begun identifying and engaging with offshore providers directly, contracting consultants as and when they need them to help negotiate contracts, or manage the transition phase once the contract has been agreed. This can be a useful tactic and can avoid taking internal resource away from the business whilst addressing many of the teething problems and change management issues common in this sort of project. SMEs should adopt a cautious approach where a provider appears to offer a quick and easy solution to their problems. Careful research and investigation of all potential offshore service providers is critical to ensuring a successful offshore engagement. Being located thousands of miles away from a supplier requires more, not less, initial scrutiny and businesses should not overlook due process when evaluating an offshore supplier.

When identifying suitable offshore providers, SMEs should first pick the country to outsource to and then select the offshore provider. The reason for this is that some countries are less stable and can leave the outsourcing company more financially exposed. Some countries also have less outsourcing experience than others and are therefore less able to offer quality services, developed infrastructure and appropriate intellectual property (IP) protection laws. Using a consultant to advise on offshore locations and help identify suitable offshore providers can save considerable time in the planning stages and ensure the long-term cost benefits from having the best fit in terms of location and supplier [see Chapter 7 for more details on location choice].

With the most suitable country identified, SMEs should draw up a list of potential offshore providers in that country, who have the required industry experience and technical skills. SMEs tend to prefer doing business with similar sized companies because they fear a loss of control from an unequal relationship. This element should also be considered when compiling the list, but should not preclude businesses that are larger (or smaller) but have a strong SME focused service offering.

Once the list is complete, an RFI (Request for Information) should be sent to each of the potential offshore providers stating the business problem and inviting proposals. The offshore provider's proposal should include:

- Response to the business problem (i.e. their proposed solution)
- Company information regarding size, structure, location, experience and capabilities
- Quality certification (e.g. ISO9001, Six Sigma)
- References and testimonials

This information will enable compilation of a shortlist of suitable providers. Ideally, face to face meetings should then be held with the shortlisted providers to explore the details of their proposal further and verify any claims. However, for most small companies this is not a realistic proposition. Many offshore providers now have local representatives who are responsible for liaising directly with potential customers in their own country. A meeting with the local representative should be used as a proxy for a country visit wherever possible. Reference to any certification or awards the offshore provider has can be a useful back-up to some of the assertions made. These also demonstrate that a provider is a serious operation that has invested for the long-term future of their business. However, it is the 'soft qualifications', such as trustworthiness, cultural fit and ways of working that are ultimately more important, although these can be extremely difficult to measure.

Caution should be paramount where suppliers make unrealistically optimistic or low bids in order to win a contract. Whilst the cost saving will look impressive in the business case, when it comes to service delivery the offshore provider will ultimately cut corners in order to maximise their cost recovery, to the detriment of the whole outsourcing relationship and offshoring programme.

The best advice is for SMEs to start with a small pilot to explore the practical issues regarding geography, service delivery and process and build momentum from there. This has the advantage of giving the SME an opportunity to evaluate some of the benefits of offshoring before becoming heavily committed. They can also get a feel for whether an offshore provider is right for them as a first step in a long-term strategy of gradual offshoring.

Larger organisations may deploy resource on permanent assignment in the offshore location to work through any of the issues that can arise during the transition phase. But for smaller firms this is less practical. An alternative is to use an experienced consultant to manage part or all of the process on the company's behalf. Finding a consultant with the right skills and experience, however, can be difficult. Most of the big consultancy firms (e.g. Accenture, IBM, CapGemini) have offshore outsourcing experts but they come at a significant premium and are often not available for smaller scale or short-term assignments. An alternative approach is to contact the National Outsourcing Association (NOA) or one of the specialist agencies who contract-out outsourcing consultants for long and short-term assignments. The cost of a consultant will vary according to experience, but is often a worthwhile investment if they can eliminate unnecessary cost and risk elsewhere in the project.

Service Level Agreements and Pricing

According to the Ventoro study [2004], in 98% of all offshore outsourcing agreements deemed to be a failure, the onshore company experienced contractual problems. That does not mean the contractual problems were the cause of failure, but they do indicate where potential issues may arise.

Service Level Agreements (SLAs) are an important component in ensuring that expectations on both sides of a relationship are clear from the outset. SLAs need to be carefully negotiated, ensuring that every detail of the outsourcing initiative is explicit and clear and that both parties have the ability and willingness to fulfill their side of the contract. Where the parties plan to share certain risks these must be carefully detailed in the SLA and closely monitored for compliance. Often companies will seek to integrate a long-term cost saving benefit, with the offshore provider taking their payment by way of incentives rather than as continuous fixed amounts. Such contracts are usually set up in such a way as to allow the offshore provider sufficient scope to be creative in the way they deliver the service. Whilst this can be a highly cost-effective way of achieving significant performance improvements, companies need to ensure that the terms of the SLA are not compromised by an offshore provider seeking to maximise cost benefits at the expense of quality. They also need to ensure that the incentives are sufficiently motivating for the offshore provider to achieve the target performance objectives.

The key principles to follow in designing any SLA are:

- Keep it simple and concise
- Establish clear roles and responsibilities for all parties
- Describe the current service / performance levels and the expected outcome as a result of the offshore arrangement in terms of tangible measures (e.g. speed, resources, quality, cycle times etc)
- Implement a performance tracking process
- Define timelines and effective dates
- Use incentives (and penalties) to drive the right behaviours
- Focus on value rather than cost
- Establish conflict resolution and escalation procedures
- Build in sufficient flexibility to allow for changes in business circumstances

The SLA should be integrated within the business contract and should not contradict the terms and conditions of the contract, particularly with reference to:

- Contract term / termination / notice periods
- Liabilities
- Intellectual Property

The principles of any pricing model should be simplicity and fairness. The offshore provider should be incentivised to provide a quality service and invest in new infrastructure to drive performance improvements, but at the same time offer ongoing value for money to the customer, balancing cost and quality.

How payment mechanisms are structured can have a considerable impact on the success of the offshoring initiative. Contracts that are set up on a 'time and materials' basis tend to have the lowest success rates (and are more open to abuse). This is because they offer no incentive to the offshore provider to improve performance or keep costs down. Fixed fee bidding is one of the most attractive approaches because it allows customers to contain their financial risk (with offshore providers covering any rising costs), however, it is only really practical where the offshore project has been clearly defined in every detail and there is little risk of unforseen changes. If not, when any change is required it could be considered 'out of scope' by the offshore provider and attract additional cost.

Managing the Offshore Provider

There are two cardinal mistakes that companies can make when managing the offshore service provider:

- They micro-manage the relationship and try to control every move the offshore service provider makes
- They pass full control of the operation over to the offshore service provider and then wash their hands of it altogether

Both approaches can have disasterous consequences. The former is likely to lead to a relationship breakdown. Overseeing all aspects of the offshore operation will be interpreted as a lack of trust in the offshore provider and may inhibit future co-operation and team building. It will also add unnecessary cost to the company. The latter can create problems if the company outsourcing the work fails to appreciate the need for ongoing relationship management and interaction with the offshore provider. Without continuous dialogue, the offshore provider is unlikely to perform the service exactly as the outsourcing company expects, no matter how clear the SLA and contract. The problem will then only manifest itself when a deadline falls due and any misunderstanding or error becomes apparent. By then it may be too late to rectify the problem, or the relationship may be irreperably damaged.

The following gives an overview of the key criteria for managing a successful outsourcer-provider relationship:

- Clarity – Discuss openly and agree expectations from the outset (including roles, responsibilities and service levels required).
- Monitor – Set realistic objectives and track them throughout the project life-cycle. Objectives should be set for both the offshore and in-house teams to ensure that maximum benefit is achieved. Monitor both 'hard' and 'soft' objectives (i.e. results and relationship).
- Contract – Put in place a contract that sets out the terms and conditions and fundamental obligations of both sides. Include incentives (and penalties) to drive the right behaviours, although caution should be used when considering penalties as they can generate conflict (under English law, certain penalties are prohibited). Likewise, incentives need to be balanced to avoid excessive risk taking which could have an adverse impact on business performance.
- Flexibility – Be prepared to accept that business circumstances change and ensure that people and systems are able to accommodate changes.
- Positive Attitude – Look for a 'win-win' outcome in every situation. This builds trust and will lead to better business performance.

Chapter 6

Why Offshoring Can Go Wrong

Whilst the opportunities for offshoring are immense, there are also many risks. In the gold rush to find significant bottom-line savings out in India and the Far East, many firms have had their fingers burnt by underestimating what it takes to be successful. Rather than saving millions, their misadventure cost them dearly and some have had to deal with the cost and embarrassment of repatriating their offshore operations.

According to the McKinsey Global Institute, up to 50% of outsourcing engagements fail to achieve their expected value. Often companies overestimate the economic benefits of the deal in their business case or fail to strike the right balance of cost and quality. In many other instances, companies have not fully engaged the necessary management resources to make the project work, or have put so much focus on getting the lowest possible price that the offshore provider is forced to reduce performance levels and contract flexibility to maintain profitability.

According to a poll by CFO magazine in 2004, the top six issues businesses consider when deciding whether or not to offshore outsource are:

1. Need to remain competitive
2. Desire to improve profit margins
3. Impact on displaced workers at the onshore operation
4. Desire to relocate resources to new opportunities
5. Impact on remaining employees morale
6. Risk of negative publicity

The arguments for and against offshore outsourcing are often focused primarily on the cost advantages and the impact on staff and public image. However, the reasons that offshore operations fail has more to do with the business model adopted, the amount of preparation done before moving offshore and the relationship with the offshore provider.

Wrong Business Model

Before embarking on an offshore programme companies must first ascertain whether offshoring is the right solution for their problem. Rather than 'jumping on the bandwagon' and following the latest offshoring trend, businesses need to objectively assess all of their options and then engage in offshoring only when it is clear there is a sustainable business benefit. A company may spend a great deal of time moving operations overseas, only to discover that the underlying cause of their problem still exists and they could have resolved the problem by improving the operation in-house. Worse still are companies that aggravate the problem by moving it overseas.

Process improvements should not be over looked when embarking on an offshore strategy. There is an old saying "rubbish-in, rubbish-out" which applies equally to offshoring. If businesses have a process that is under-performing and want to outsource it (sometimes described as "do my mess for less"), they should also look at opportunities to apply best practice techniques to the process before sending it overseas. This way they can maximise the benefit they will get back from the offshore provider both in terms of higher productivity and lower cost. Again, a good consultant can help in redesigning and improving operations prior to transition.

Businesses should consider offshoring as a long-term business strategy rather than a short-term fix to an internal problem. If a company embarks on offshoring as a twelve-month cost cutting exercise they are more likely to fail than if they take a long-term strategic view. This is because their expectations are less likely to be met if the project has a short life and there is less incentive for the offshore provider to commit to the outsourcer's business in terms of investment or quality resources.

Planning & Preparation

Often companies fail to grasp that offshore outsourcing requires a great deal of prior planning and preparation in order to achieve success. This involves clearly defining the processes, activities and performance expectations that are required, selecting the right provider, engaging with them to verify that every detail has been understood and can be executed correctly and tying down the roles and responsibilities of each party during the contract.

Relationship Management

Outsourcing relationships commonly fail because:

- Insufficient resource is committed to relationship management
- Internal management skills are inadequate to manage the relationship
- Expected benefits are unrealistic, generating conflict

Relationship breakdowns need to be anticipated in advance and appropriately covered by well-designed exit strategies (this should cover the transfer and repatriation of intellectual property). However, businesses also need recognise the necessity to change the way they behave in order to make the relationship work. By pursuing an offshore outsourcing strategy, they must move from being an owner of the process to an owner of the policy and scope of the outsourcing agreement. They must go from being a service deliverer to a supplier manager or a business partner facilitating the offshore arrangement. They should aim to develop long-term relationships with offshore providers which:

- Develop and promote trust between each side and adopt a 'team' approach
- Encourage continuous improvement for mutual benefit
- Provide clarity of roles, responsibilities and expectations for behaviour
- Enhance credibility by setting and demonstrating consistent standards

Risk to Innovation

A concern for businesses making a long-term commitment to offshoring arrangements is the impact on the innovation process. It has often been argued that outsourcing can lead to greater innovation by freeing resources to work on value-creating activities. This is supported by the fact that businesses gain access to specialist skills and knowledge through outsourcing that they do not possess within their own organisations. However, over-reliance on external companies can lead to an erosion of internal knowledge and skills, transfer the benefits of organisational learning to the outsourcing provider and reduce investment in internal research and development. Outsourcing is sometimes seen as a "quick fix" solution to adopt rather than developing new ideas and innovations. This is referred to as a "hollowing-out" effect where the organisation's learning and new technology capabilities become depleted [Odindo et al]. SMEs especially need to be aware of the capabilities they transfer (or lose) to outsourcing providers. They need to establish safeguards to ensure that innovation and organisational learning is enhanced, not depleted, as a result of outsourcing. The outsourcing relationship should emphasise shared learning, a commitment to continuous improvement and ongoing investment in new technologies. An ability to reintegrate the outsourced activity may also be advisable if it is of strategic importance.

A further concern with outsourcing is the potential loss of cross-functional team skills. Often it is these skills that can generate new ideas, new ways of working and product innovations. Outsourcing can limit the opportunity for cross-functional interaction and thereby stifle the innovation process. Companies should maintain regular dialogue and strong relationships with offshore providers in order to engender co-operation and team working across the organisations.

Loss of Control

Loss of control is usually one of the biggest concerns for any SME looking at outsourcing. It can come about because the company does not have the capability, time or experience to effectively manage the outsourcing provider. Smaller companies may also feel intimidated working with larger businesses (as outsourcing providers often are) and fear that their unequal size may lead to a loss of control.

Often smaller businesses are controlled by a business owner or a handful of shareholders who have a long association with the business and are used to controlling all aspects of the operation themselves. Relinquishing some of that control in the name of greater productivity and lower cost is often very difficult emotionally. Where externally handled information is sensitive (e.g. in the case of customer or financial data), this issue is very often magnified. The distance in time and geography which are an integral part of offshoring adds to the perceived risk.

The loss of IP is often the number one worry of those who are offshore outsourcing. There have been several high-profile cases where employees of Indian outsourcing companies sold confidential information to third parties, undermining public and business confidence and causing significant damage to the industry's image. Whilst it is fair to say that such cases are very isolated and could possibly have happened in the U.K. or U.S. with an on-shore outsourcing company, they serve to underline the need to be vigilant and put in place proper security procedures. It is important to appoint reputable service providers with appropriate safeguards and security measures to ensure that operations overseas meet the standards required by businesses and customers in the West.

Research by consulting group Ventoro, in 2004 found that as many as one in ten firms experience IP theft during their offshore projects. However, the surprising finding is not the scale of the IP problem but the source of it – onshore employees are twice as likely to steal confidential material than the offshore team. The research indicated that the problem is caused by onshore employees feeling alienated from the company as a result of the offshoring initiative. The research also found that the impact of offshore theft tends to be more limited that the impact of onshore theft. The most damaging IP theft incidents have occurred in the U.S. or Europe. The reason being that the market for such information is more developed in the U.S. and Europe and the theft damage is likely to spread more quickly.

Business control can actually be enhanced by outsourcing. A 2005 study by Accenture and The Economist Intelligence Unit found that 43% of finance managers who had outsourced activities in their company believed that outsourcing actually improved control and governance in their business. This is because outsourced processes are usually better designed and documented than processes which remain in-house and are underpinned by SLAs and performance measures which very often enhance the control and management of those processes. In addition, they felt that it was easier to stay on top of tax and regulatory changes because of greater transparency of information.

Offshore outsourcing relationships should be structured to ensure that they retain the right level of control for the company outsourcing, especially where any decision can affect the company directly. This clearly needs to be balanced with the higher costs that greater control brings.

Negative Publicity

Over the past couple of years, SMEs have tended to avoid offshoring due to fears of bad publicity. The fear of negative public relations with local communities and the fear of competitors using their decision to offshore as a way of discrediting them have outweighed the potential benefits.

However, there are signs that the political environment for offshoring may be changing and becoming more accepting as companies increasingly push to remain competitive in the face of growing global competition. The key to managing PR on the issue is to be open about the fact that the company is offshoring jobs and to communicate the benefits. Communication should include:

- The financial benefits (and therefore future profits) to shareholders
- The need to remain competitive to secure a sustainable future to employees
- The need to continuously improve productivity and performance to provide a better service to customers

Businesses that avoid open communication on the issue are more likely to face a public backlash later, if and when the move becomes public. They are also more likely to be the subject of misleading publicity or rumours. This then reflects badly on the company, as it appears they are concealing a bad decision, which in turn can alienate customers, staff and local communities who are often crucial to making the process of offshoring work.

Businesses that have fully investigated the process and have sound and compelling business reasons to move their work overseas, will often find that communicating the facts openly can build respect for their decision. It is important, however, that communication is not shrouded in confusing business jargon as this can be off-putting for customers and staff and again make it appear that the company has something to hide. Even the expression "offshoring" can appear Machiavellian to some and is better replaced with a clear explanation of what the business is doing.

Job losses for SMEs as a result of offshoring tend to be less of a threat than for large firms, because offshoring is often used as a way to access more resource to generate growth, rather than to simply reduce head-count. It can also complement local employee skills, by allowing on-shore workers to concentrate on higher value-adding activities such as improving core products or customer service and driving business performance. This fact should be stressed in any communication particularly where offshoring will not result in redundancies.

Wage Inflation

Research on the impact of offshoring on wage levels in provider countries is still fairly limited. However, there is a fear that increased offshoring activity in cities such as Bangalore and Mumbai have accelerated wage inflation by over 13% per annum and that in the next few years any cost advantages of offshoring could disappear.

There are several reasons to believe this will not happen. Local wage inflation (and real-estate price increases) will continue in certain offshoring locations while multinationals companies focus demand on two or three major cities in India. The sunk costs in setting up large offshore operations mean that such businesses cannot quickly switch away from these hot spots. However, as businesses become more confident about offshoring and the appropriate infrastructure (particularly telecommunications and technology access) becomes more available and widespread, many companies will begin to disperse their demand to other Indian cities and other provider countries such as China, Bangladesh and Sri Lanka. At the same time, the attractiveness of the offshore sector for many graduates in provider countries will ensure that the supply of quality talent continues to grow for the foreseeable future, keeping rising prices in check.

According to a study by The McKinsey Global Institute [2005], although wages in offshore markets will probably rise, they are unlikely to reach the level of wages in the developed markets.

Business Continuity

There is a significant risk that staff, suppliers and customers do not support the business during the transition to an offshore business model. Offshore strategies are intrinsically difficult to manage and success requires the goodwill of all stakeholders.

Customer attrition is a key area of concern. Any business lost as a result of offshoring is a cost to the project and can be crippling for a small company - quickly undermining any potential cost savings that have been identified. An important step, as part of the initial preparation and building of the business case, is to understand the customer's perspective, particularly if they are likely to be affected in any way by the offshoring initiative. It is common for customers to initially state their opposition to offshoring on principle. However, understanding their underlying concerns will enable the company to adapt the business model and provide reassurance.

One way to do this is to ask customers whether they would be prepared to pay a premium for a locally delivered solution. If the answer is "yes", then offshoring is probably not a recommended approach. However, research shows that this is unlikely to be the case and cost will ultimately be the key consideration. This does, however, demonstrate the importance of listening carefully to customers to understand their real motivations. A further consideration is whether there are any practical factors making offshoring a non-starter (e.g. legal, regulatory or physical obstacles to the customer using the offshore service). Detailed understanding of customers will highlight the majority of these factors where they exist.

Uncertainty during transition can significantly increase the risk of staff turnover, so companies need to communicate plans to staff from the early stages and design retention programmes that target key personnel. Change management techniques are valuable in ensuring that employees support any offshoring initiative and can actively participate in the process. These techniques include:

- Providing a formal business approach to manage the change (rather than reacting to individual cases)
- Ensuring a single, clear message from senior management
- Communication that confronts business reality and provides a compelling case for change
- Monitoring morale within the organisation and adapting the message accordingly
- Engaging directly with individuals to explain how the change will affect them personally

A common staff problem is the increase in competition between onshore and offshore teams. On the one hand offshore teams may push for more responsibilities and work. On the other onshore teams will want to prove their worth and may seek to undermine the offshore team. Actively managing the team dynamic (e.g. staff motivation, incentives, etc) to ensure that all staff understand the benefits and support the bigger company picture will minimise the risk.

For suppliers, the key concern will be the potential loss of business that could result from the move to an offshore provider, especially where their products or services are complementary. During the transition phase their support will be crucial in ensuring business continuity. The company should ensure that the supplier relationship is maintained throughout the project, keeping them informed of developments and providing sufficient incentives to continue supply (e.g. through contracts and retention bonuses).

One way of reducing risk to business continuity is by running small pilot trials of the processes or projects to be offshored, before rolling out the operation on a wider scale.

Measuring Progress

Measuring the progress of an offshore project is a key component in ensuring success. This is an area that many larger firms often neglect. They may budget and track the direct costs and benefits, but don't necessarily have clarity on the indirect costs. Smaller companies are often better at monitoring the impact of offshoring than their larger counterparts because their scale and business culture tends to focus on cash-flow and accounting for 'pounds and pennies'. There is often more transparency on the impact of offshored projects and operations in a small company than there might be in a large corporation.

Reducing Risk

Embarking on an outsourcing relationship is essentially an exercise in risk management. It is concerned with maximising the upside benefits from the outsourcing agreement, whilst minimising the risks. Identifying risks at the beginning, understanding them and tracking them throughout the life of an offshore initiative is one of the most effective ways to reducing them. Reduced risks mean that a company can lower its costs and increase the chances of success.

By following a systematic risk mapping exercise [like the 'risk matrix'], companies can quickly identify where resource and time should be focused to mitigate or even eliminate a risk.

The Risk Matrix

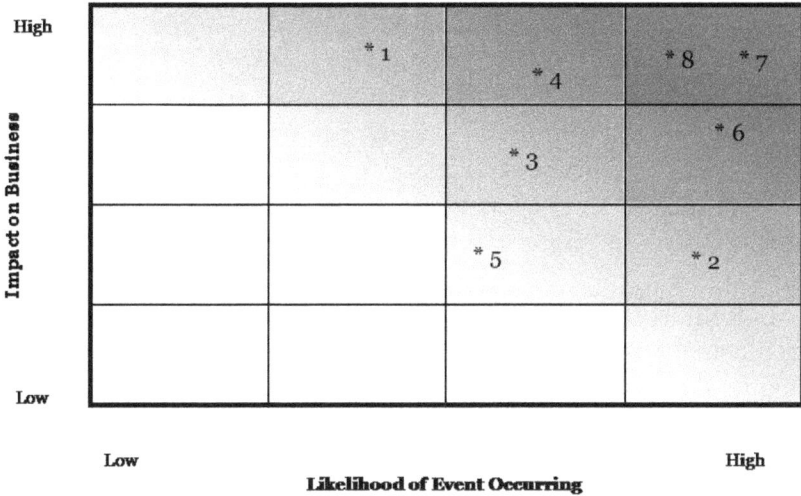

Risk matrix plotting "Impact on Business" (Low to High, vertical axis) against "Likelihood of Event Occurring" (Low to High, horizontal axis), with items *1, *4, *8, *7, *6, *3, *5, *2 plotted.

Risks (examples)

Business Case	1. Lack of key stakeholder support
	2. Underestimating wage inflation in India
Infrastructure	3. Delay in upgrading local telecoms network
	4. Office space unavailable – delay of >three months
Transition	5. Cultural & communication issues
	6. Failure to meet quality targets
People	7. Retention of key staff
	8. Ability to recruit sufficient calibre / quantity of staff

The Robinson Partnership – Case Study

When The Robinson Partnership*, a medium-sized accountancy practice in the South-East of England, found themselves experiencing chronic staff shortages and a back-log of client work in January 2005, they saw two options: either turn to their traditional recruitment agent to find more part-qualified accountants or book-keepers, or make a strategic change and try offshore outsourcing.

The Robinson Partnership were aware that it was becoming increasingly difficult to find the right calibre of person to do their client's day-to-day book-keeping, while remaining profitable. At their standard hourly rate to clients, they were just about breaking-even but recognised that they needed to offer their clients the book-keeping service in order to gain the higher margin advisory revenues which actually made their business profitable. They were looking for a long-term solution that would deliver a step-change in their business performance, whilst overcoming the issues of staff turnover, rising costs and low profitability.

Having heard about the growing trend towards offshore outsourcing The Robinson Partnership were keen to find out more, but were worried about the process and risks to their business: how would they go about setting it up; who would manage the process for them; how could they ensure the quality of the work when not in direct control of the process ?

The Robinson Partnership decided to contact Outspan Consulting to find out more about their business process outsourcing service, called "Business First". After an initial consultation they decided to trial the service using one of their client's accounts from a previous quarter. This gave them the opportunity to evaluate the benefits of offshoring for themselves on a low-risk basis, whilst having a reliable benchmark against which to compare the results.

Outspan Consulting collected the paperwork from their offices and scanned the documents into electronic format for processing in India. The Indian team reconciled the paperwork and provided confirmation back of the information they had received. The data was processed according to The Robinson Partnership's requirements and quality checked by a Chartered Accountant in India to ensure that all records had been accounted for correctly. Once completed, the team produced an electronic file of the processed data for The Robinson Partnership to upload into their software and a CD-ROM of all the scanned images of their client's paperwork, making it quick and easy for them to retrieve any documents they wanted to review in more detail.

The trial gave The Robinson Partnership the confidence that offshoring would meet their high quality standards whilst delivering significant cost advantages. It also opened-up a new pool of resources they could call upon to meet ongoing changes in their business needs. The trial demonstrated to The Robinson Partnership that they could reduce their costs by 60%, redeploy their existing staff, take on new clients and increase their time spent on business advisory services. On the basis of this positive experience they decided to engage Outspan Consulting as outsource service provider for book-keeping and monthly reporting of their clients accounts.

The first step in setting-up the process ongoing involved a one-to-one session to understand each client's business, their accounting requirements and their transaction history. Next Outspan Consulting assessed each client's process requirements and identified areas where the process could be improved using best practice principles in order to enhance efficiency and productivity. This meant that the client would achieve even greater savings on their processing cost, by significantly improving the way the data was being handled and processed. The final stage in the set-up process was to establish the Service Level Agreement for each client's account to include their required data format, timescales and performance standards.

Having completed this exercise, Outspan Consulting were able to compile a business case highlighting the cost saving opportunities for The Robinson Partnership and a quote for processing their clients work on an ongoing basis.

Outspan Consulting began processing The Robinson Partnership's client accounts under a long-term contract. Clients were now getting a better service from their accountant and, with a more flexible business model, the accountancy practice were able to take on more new clients by offering the most competitive prices for book-keeping and monthly reporting services. This in turn led to more opportunities to sell-on higher margin advisory services and overall increased profitability. The business expects to be offshoring 25% of their client's book-keeping operations by the end of the year and all of their clients by the end of 2006.

Name changed for confidentiality

Chapter 7

Making Your Move - The Practicalities of Offshoring for SMEs

How to chose an offshore location

Different businesses have different needs from their offshore operations, driven by differences in their business model (both in terms of the future scale of their operations and whether they plan to set up a captive arrangement or outsource to a third-party provider). With a variety of different needs, businesses will tend to evaluate the costs and benefits of the same location in different ways.

Determining the right offshore location for a business can be difficult. Many SMEs often don't spend sufficient time evaluating location. Decisions are driven by the best price, with little consideration given to where the offshore operations may be located. However, this has the potential to store problems for the future. If the offshore provider is located in a city experiencing high labour demand, the likelihood of increased wages and high staff turnover will inevitably have an impact on prices and service performance in due course. Companies need to assess the location of potential offshore operations before committing to any one offshore provider, including the supply of suitable labour and the real cost of employing it. To determine the suitability of each potential offshore location, companies must clearly define their business needs. As a minimum this should include:

- Cost
- Quality of offshore providers

- Quality of offshore infrastructure
- Business & economic environment
- Risk profile (political and security)

Each factor should be weighted according to business objectives. Data can then be gathered on each of the potential locations in order to calculate a preference index ranking countries / locations according to the business' objectives.

An example of this can be seen below [score 1 to 10 : where 1 is the most attractive location, 10 is the least attractive]

Weighting	*50%*	*20%*	*10%*	*10%*	*10%*	
	Cost	Quality of Offshore Providers	Offshore Infrastructure Quality	Business & Economic Environ.	Risk Profile	Location Preference Index
India	1	1	10	9	7	**3.3**
China	2	4	2	10	9	**3.9**
Philippines	3	6	4	8	10	**4.9**
Malaysia	4	10	3	7	3	**5.3**
Hungary	5	8	6	3	5	**5.5**
Ireland	9	2	5	1	1	**5.6**
Netherlands	10	3	1	2	2	**6.1**
Poland	7	5	7	5	6	**6.3**
Czech Rep	6	9	8	4	4	**6.4**
Russia	8	7	9	6	8	**7.7**

This template can be used to compare city locations either within countries or across multiple countries to enhance the location selection process.

The Economist Intelligence Unit's study [2005] ranked the following countries in order of offshoring attractiveness (score in brackets):

1. India (7.76)
2. China (7.34)
3. Czech Republic (7.26)
4. Singapore (7.25)
5. Poland (7.24)
6. Canada (7.23)
7. Hong Kong (7.19)
8. Hungary (7.17)
9. Philippines (7.17)
10. Thailand (7.16)

This score was based on nine different criteria (relative weighting in brackets): labour costs (0.3), labour skills (0.3), labour regulation (0.1), proximity to major sources of investment (0.05), political and security risk (0.05), macroeconomic stability (0.05), regulatory environment (0.05), tax regime (0.05) and infrastructure (0.05).

Indian Take-Away

Whilst there is a wide choice of offshore locations, many businesses that are new to offshore outsourcing choose India, China or The Philippines – predominantly because labour costs are so low. Of these three, India usually comes out top because of its abundant supply of English-speaking labour and cultural links to the Anglo-Saxon world. In the past few years, development of offshore outsourcing in India has been concentrated in six main cities – Bangalore, Mumbai (Bombay), Chennai (Madras), Pune, New Delhi, Kolkata (Calcutta) [see Appendix for more details on each city]. Of these six, Bangalore is the most popular.

Bangalore is often referred to as the 'Silicon Valley of India'. It is widely regarded as the centre of India's IT sector and has witnessed a transformation both in economic growth and business image over the past ten years. It is now considered one of the country's most attractive IT destinations with a large number of education and research institutions, good telecoms infrastructure, a high standard of living, availability of quality office space and positive investor image.

However, a closer look at the alternatives shows that Bangalore (or even India) is not the only choice when it comes to location.

At present the IT / Business Process Outsourcing (BPO) industry in India is experiencing its third wave of growth. The first wave was characterised by large multinationals such as GE, American Express and Swiss Air setting up captive operations in India. In the second wave, growth was predominantly generated by entrepreneurs (often ex-employees of multinationals) setting up their own IT businesses. The third wave is much more geographically dispersed with new offshoring locations starting to emerge – often referred to as 'Tier Two' cities. This new phase is being driven by a number of elements:

- Companies have sought alternative locations to reduce their exposure to a particular city and reduce the risks to business continuity

- Improvements have been made to infrastructure (telecoms, energy and real estate) in many new locations

- Cost of labour and real estate are lower in Tier Two cities

- State governments have created favourable policy environments and incentives to attract investment

Bangalore is likely to continue to boom in the coming years, but there is evidence that other states are now working hard to capture some of the growth of the IT / BPO outsourcing industry. This has sparked a friendly rivalry between the various states in India, with cities such as Ahmedabad, Chandigarh, Jaipur and more recently, Cochin joining the race.

As for the fourth wave – this may come in the shape of 'digital villages' or 'high-tech communities'. For years, India's software and outsourcing services boom has centred on a handful of 'cyber-cities', experiencing spectacular growth and increases in wealth whilst all around the rest of the country has remained relatively untouched. The outsourcing phenomenon has the potential to reach even the smallest of communities and create thousands of jobs, new opportunities for development and widespread improvements in standards of living for the 300 million middle class Indians spread across the country.

China versus India?

China has received a great deal of press coverage in recent times as a potential rival to India's number one position in the offshore outsourcing league. However, whilst it has several attractions (not least an abundance of low cost labour), there are good reasons to believe that India will continue to hold on to its leadership position over the next ten years:

- Lack of English language skills is one of the biggest obstacles to the growth of the outsourcing industry in China. English is essential for every offshoring project - from call centres to software development. On this point alone, India has an enormous advantage with over two million English-speaking graduates joining the labour market each year. The Chinese government has recognised the problem and is investing more than $5.4 billion in English education at universities.

- Culturally China is more alien to western cultures than India. The legacy of British colonialism has endowed India with an education, legal and political system that makes it easier for Indian and Western companies to understand each other. China's legal and tax systems differ across the various provinces, creating additional complexity and cost. There are signs that China is starting to integrate further with Western cultures through its preparations for the 2008 Beijing Olympics and admission to the World Trade Organisation, but India still holds a stronger position when it comes to cultural and legal fit.

- Costs tend to be similar in both countries with the exception of real estate and energy costs which are lower in China

- China has a labour pool of over 200,000 IT professionals and 50,000 new graduates joining the market each year. Although Chinese universities excel in technical subjects, many graduates migrate to the U.S. / Europe where they can earn substantially higher wages. In this respect India leads the world with nearly 500,000 IT graduates joining the Indian labour market each year

- India has almost 80% of global BPO revenues. This has enabled the industry to build scale and develop world-class operations and best practice customer relationship management. China's offshore outsourcing industry, by contrast, is still relatively underdeveloped and highly fragmented into a large number of small players. Their ability to attract large-scale projects has been limited by the lack of scale and experience of individual providers in the market. However, China is catching up fast - lowering costs by scaling up operations.

- Even if China can't match India, it may be able to take a substantial share of the global BPO market. China has a lead over India in terms of quality telecoms infrastructure, roads and government support.

A likely scenario is that global firms wishing to outsource will adopt India for service-based work (e.g. call centres, software development and transaction processing) and China for manufacturing (e.g. cheap PCs, processing chips and other hardware-manufactured items).

The Best of The Rest

The Philippines

- Cost is on a par with China (technical salaries in the range $5,000 to $10,000 per annum; back-office from $3,000 to $10,000 p.a.)
- Large pool of well-qualified English speaking labour (380,000 graduates annually – 15,000 focused on technology subjects)
- Low staff turnover
- Strong cultural affinity with the U.S. (including U.S. accounting and customer service standards)
- Offshoring activity now spreading to locations beyond Manila
- Government exemptions available from export taxes, fees, dues and licences for operations opened in new IT parks
- Reliable telecoms infrastructure (legacy of U.S. military bases)
- Political stability questionable
- High levels of corruption
- Major Customers: American International Group, Citigroup, Procter & Gamble

Malaysia

- Well-educated, multi-lingual work force (most graduates fluent in English; 75,000 IT and engineering graduates annually)
- Costs relatively low
- Politically relatively stable
- Government policy of positioning Malaysia as a hub for services and technology innovation
- Major Customers: HSBC, Electronic Data Systems, Motorola, Prudential, Ericsson, IBM

Russia

- Third largest population of engineers and scientists per capita
- English language skills poor
- IT salaries range from $5,000 to $10,000
- Back-office processing industry is still underdeveloped
- Infrastructure quality and availability reasonable inside one of Russia's few IT parks, but poor elsewhere
- Telecoms infrastructure costs above average
- Government unpredictable and not particularly business-friendly – no real incentives for offshore working
- Major Customers: Boeing

Mexico

- Number one location for Spanish-speaking contact centres, but poor English language skills
- Labour costs approximately 50% lower than in the U.S..
- Infrastructure reliable inside the technology parks but unreliable elsewhere
- Government does not offer particularly attractive incentives for offshoring work
- Major Customers: General Motors, IBM, AOL Time Warner

Ireland

- Labour pool relatively small, but highly educated and English speaking (34,000 graduates annually, 5,000 technical)
- Labour and capital costs relatively high (technical salaries range from $25,000 to $40,000)
- Solid infrastructure
- Favourable tax laws
- €300 million technology-education fund providing incentives
- Major Customers: Dell, Microsoft, Intel

A Comparison of Labour Cost versus Labour Pool Attractiveness

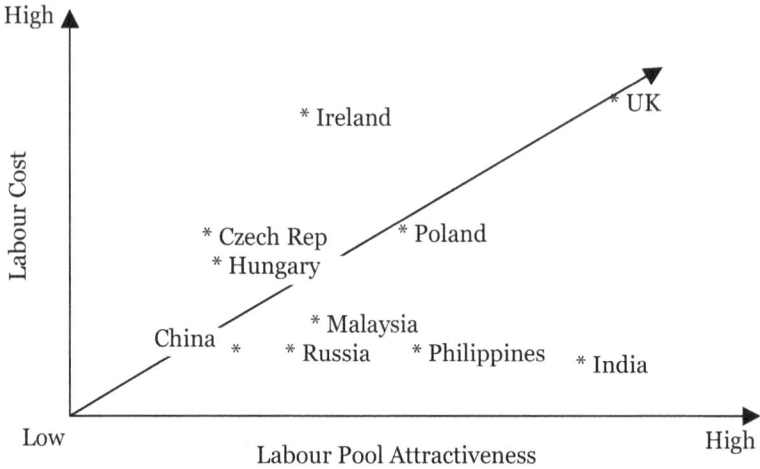

High ▲ Labour Cost

* Ireland

* UK

* Czech Rep   * Poland
* Hungary

China *   * Malaysia
              * Russia   * Philippines   * India

Low   Labour Pool Attractiveness   High

Based on assessment of actual labour cost data / quality and size of labour pool – Aug 2005

On the basis of this analysis, India offers the best combination of available, qualified staff at lowest cost.

Lost in Translation – Cultural Issues

Cultural factors should not be underestimated in the success of offshore projects. Many companies make the mistake of assuming that because they are the customer, the offshore provider and their team should adapt their culture, working practices and business values. Likewise, onshore teams are not always accepting of the offshore provider's culture and a certain amount of 'cultural friction' and misunderstanding may arise. Many companies ignore cultural issues altogether, assuming that culture has no effect on offshore projects.

Companies should always seek to understand and be comfortable with the local business culture and that of the offshore provider before embarking on an offshoring project or commitment. Ultimately, the only real way to understand another business culture is to spend time experiencing it first hand. For many SMEs this is not always practical, but they can develop their understanding by interacting with the offshore provider via phone, e-mail and small-scale trials, prior to engaging on a permanent, large-scale basis.

Whilst it is not possible to describe the cultural issues that companies are likely to experience for each and every offshore destination, there are certain characteristics of the Indian market (the largest of the destination for offshore service provision) that can provide a useful insight:

- The Indian education system places a heavy emphasis on rote learning, which produces logical, practical minds rather than creative lateral thinkers. Indian business people with a higher education, however, are better at thinking analytically
- The boss takes all responsibility for decision-making. As a result, employees are reticent to accept responsibility.
- Employees follow instructions without questioning them. They do not argue even if they know the boss is wrong.
- Indians are often too polite to directly answer "no". They will tend to give evasive answers such as "I'll try" and "Perhaps" rather than "No, it's impossible".
- Indians tend to avoid conflict and consider loss of temper as a weakness. Maintaining composure and being patient in business dealings is essential to achieve progress.
- Delays are part of life in India and are to be expected in business, particularly when dealing with government and officials. Realistic timescales are crucial.

More generic advice for offshoring projects in other cultures:

- Adjust management style to accommodate cultural differences.
- Embrace cultural differences – it can make doing business more interesting and diverse and could even generate new ideas and ways of working.
- Be consistent in dealings with onshore and offshore teams – nothing is more likely to raise tensions than if one side is being treated differently than the other.
- Monitor the state of the relationship and tackle conflict before it arises.

Impact on the Onshore Team

Clearly for any company that plans to replace onshore resources with offshore employees, there will be a direct impact on the onshore team and any employees rendered redundant. This is true even where resources are redeployed. Often companies instigate retraining schemes to enable displaced workers either to find new employment or take on work elsewhere in the business. This can be highly beneficial for the individual, who gains new skills and enhanced marketability, as well as the company who can redeploy the employee to higher value work. If the employee is exiting the business, retraining demonstrates the company's commitment to treating all employees fairly.

Employee redeployment is not always feasible, however. Where a displaced resource has been working in an unskilled area (e.g. call centre, customer support, etc), it is usually fairly practical to retrain them to work in another low-skilled area of the business. Where the resource has come from a relatively skilled area (e.g. software programming), it is often much harder and more costly to retrain them to work in an alternative skilled area (e.g. project manager). Different jobs require different experiences and personalities and an individual who is comfortable working in one area may feel completely demotivated if redeployed in another area, even if the two areas may appear fairly complementary.

The impact on the rest of the team, even if they are not directly affected, must also be considered. They are likely to feel threatened, possibly demotivated and often quite uncomfortable if parts of the business are being outsourced to offshore locations. Businesses must take proactive steps to manage employees that remain in the business and allay any concerns that they have. This should include:

- A clearly defined plan for the ongoing business showing where each individual fits.
- Regular, honest and open communication to ensure that employees feel involved in the process and can raise any queries or concerns.

- Career development plans with clear objectives and deliverables so that each individual can contribute to the success of the offshore programme and the overall business.
- Training programmes, where appropriate, to ensure that employees have the right skills and to demonstrate a long-term investment in their future.

Companies should regularly monitor morale and adapt motivation techniques and retention plans according to changing circumstances.

Data Protection

The decision to offshore usually entails some sort of transfer of personal data. U.S. and European legislation regulates the transfer of such data (e.g. the U.K. Data Protection Act 1998) and is often perceived as highly restrictive. Companies dislike of data restrictions are matched only by consumer fears about abuse of personal data by fraudsters and unscrupulous marketers.

So, what is the position for small companies looking to pursue an offshoring strategy, but unsure about their legal obligations?

Contrary to popular belief, the Data Protection Act in the EU does not preclude companies from sending data to countries outside the EU. The main clause relating to such transfers is known as the eighth data principle and states that *"personal data shall not be transferred to a country or territory outside the European Economic Area unless that country or territory ensures an adequate level of protection for the rights and freedoms of data subjects in relation to the processing of personal data"*. The key is in establishing the adequacy of data protection in the offshore destination country.

The EU has already declared some countries as having an adequate level of protection. Australia, Canada, Guernsey, Hong Kong, the Isle of Man, Israel, Japan, Jersey, New Zealand, Switzerland and Taiwan all meet the required levels. India, however, does not have the levels of legal data protection mandated by the EU, although new legislation is expected.

However, it is still possible to demonstrate adequacy, even for countries that have not been officially sanctioned by the EU. This can be done by:

- **Self-assessment** : The EU Information Commissioner has set guidelines to enable data controllers to satisfy themselves that data being transferred to another country has adequate levels of protection. The guidelines relate to the nature of data being transferred, how the data will be used and the laws and practices of the destination country.
- **Exceptions** : The eighth data principle will not apply outside the EU where the data controller has obtained express consent from the data subject. This consent has to be given freely and without duress.
- **Group Companies**: Where the outsourcing is between multinational companies in the same group, it is possible to have a binding agreement that stipulates privacy compliance throughout the group.
- **U.S. Safe Harbor**: a special arrangement for the U.S. has been made called 'The Safe Harbor System'. Where a company publicly discloses a commitment to the Safe Harbor rules and subjects itself to the authority of the Federal Trade Commission, it is deemed to comply with the rules of adequacy.

Once adequacy has been established, a company needs to ascertain whether it, or the offshore provider, is the data controller. Where the offshore provider receives data as the data controller then it will need to ensure that it is in compliance with the Act directly. Where the offshore provider is simply a data processor on behalf of its client, then it is the client who is the data controller and must ensure that they have consent from their customers to process their data outside the EU.

Once responsibility for data control has been established, a company that intends to process personal data outside the EU needs to ensure that they comply with the seventh data principle (set out in Schedule 1 Part I of the Data Protection Act) which requires that " *appropriate technical and organisational measures shall be taken against unauthorised or unlawful processing of personal data and against accidental loss or destruction of, or damage to, personal data."* This implies that the data controller:

- Obtains sufficient guarantees that security measures are in place to safeguard data.
- Takes all reasonable steps to ensure compliance with all principles.
- Retains overall control of the data and the data processor (i.e. the offshore service provider) acts only in accordance with instructions from the data controller (as specified explicitly by contract).

Providing that the data controller agrees and enforces the seventh data principle requirements in the contract, compliance with the Act is achieved.

The Data Protection Act continues to be a source of concern for companies looking at offshore outsourcing. However, providing they have taken reasonable steps to ensure compliance and have set up an appropriate contract with the offshore outsourcing company, there is no reason why it should present an obstacle to pursuing an offshore strategy.

Chapter 8

The Road Ahead

In the mid 1990s, the new digital era was born. Web browsers brought digital connectivity to the masses which then led to standard, Web-based software applications that created whole new business models and businesses, such as eBay. The peer-to-peer "open-software" phenomenon that quickly followed then produced further advances in on-line collaboration through file sharing, Voice Over Internet Protocol (VOIP) and on-demand software. These new technologies helped push outsourcing to new levels allowing a vast array of processes and projects to be more independent of location than ever before, creating truly "global supply chains" and new opportunities for businesses and individuals to interact on a massive scale.

So what is next for the burgeoning offshore industry? What future trends are emerging and how will the industry change in the next five years?

1. The scope of offshoring will increase – while IT and business processes have to date been the most heavily outsourced functions, companies are increasingly comfortable outsourcing their higher value operations overseas. Functions such as finance, accounting, procurement and HR will become the focus of offshoring initiatives, with recruitment, pension planning and analytical activities all considered viable for offshoring to specialist providers.

2. Changing definition of core business – companies have tended not to outsource core competencies in the past. Whilst this trend is expected to continue for the foreseeable future, the definition of what is core is likely to come under closer scrutiny and some redefinition. For example, in the

past a company may have described product design, or budgeting and forecasting as core activities. However, with growing demands elsewhere in the business to focus resources only on those activities that clearly create consumer preference or can command a higher price in the market, a company may judge that an outside provider will handle these activities better and at lower cost. The key is to be selective about what to keep in house and what can go offshore.

3. The shape of organisations will change – along with a redefinition of what is core and non-core and greater competition in each area of the business value-chain, will come the need to collaborate more effectively with other businesses to remain competitive. This will give rise to the 'virtual organisation' where a cluster of different suppliers come together to produce for different sets of customers, according to their needs. This will require greater organisational flexibility, but at a cost. Businesses will lose direct control over many activities as more and more elements of the value chain become outsourced. Supplier management will therefore become a core competence and competitive advantage will be gained by those organisations that can best co-ordinate their portfolio of suppliers.

4. Recruiting staff will become increasingly difficult – the so-called 'war for talent' will increase as the effect of an ageing population in the West takes its toll. At the same time many more people will seek to retire earlier to enjoy a better lifestyle and decreasing job security will drive individuals to "binge work" (i.e. sell their skills on the open market to the highest bidder, staying with a firm for a limited period before moving on). Companies will be forced to look further afield to attract the right talent and will need to adopt new working practices and flexible organisational boundaries to recruit outside their traditional labour pool.

5. SMEs will increasingly access offshore services via the Internet – with greater access to technology and falling communications costs, SMEs will be able to access a growing range of sophisticated software and business systems via the

Internet. Many of these systems will be available on a metered 'per usage' basis, rather than through expensive fixed licence agreements making them more accessible and cost effective to even the smallest business. This, in turn, will allow more SMEs to take advantage of offshoring by combining systems that can be accessed from any location with service provision from an offshore provider. An example of this is where Outspan Consulting provides accounting services to its clients in the U.K. from an offshore centre in India via a shared server. Clients can access their information on customised versions of SAP, Sage and many other software packages via a secure link on the Internet, at any time or place.

6. <u>A better political environment for offshoring</u> – as the wider economic benefits of greater competitiveness become more apparent, the political environment will become more accepting of offshoring. Governments will still need to assist displaced workers in finding alternative work and overcome any short-term political backlash, but the benefits of a vibrant, competitive economy will assist in resisting calls for protectionist policies.

7. <u>Growing importance in the public sector</u> – as budgets continue to come under pressure in local and national governments, the need to offshore outsource will become unavoidable. The adoption of Public Finance Initiatives (PFI) to fund public projects in the U.K., for example, is already blurring the boundary between public and private and will increasingly involve an element of offshoring to overcome tighter funding conditions.

Conclusion

Many small businesses are starting to recognise the possibilities of offshore outsourcing. They are increasingly aware of the strategic benefits and know that by not outsourcing certain activities they will need to continue costly local investment in people, training, research and development and systems for long periods to run those activities efficiently. They are also beginning to acknowledge that offshoring drives competitive advantage and if they do not start seriously evaluating it for themselves, they may soon become uncompetitive.

As offshore providers continue to target smaller businesses and technology and communication costs continue to fall, it is likely that SMEs will adopt offshoring in ever greater numbers. The global offshore services market is expected to be worth in excess of $250 billion by 2008 (representing an average of 40% growth year on year since 1998). A substantial part of this new growth will come from the SME sector.

Whilst there has been a lot of negative publicity surrounding offshoring, many SMEs have realised that by adopting an offshore strategy, they are able to access new resources and skills and redeploy their existing employees on higher value activities. Rather than creating mass redundancies, offshoring is helping these companies to improve their performance and free themselves from growth constraints.   By being smart and doing things more efficiently and cost effectively these businesses are demonstrating to staff, suppliers, customers, peers and investors that they are 'leading-edge'.   It is also enabling them to be more competitive, more innovative and ultimately more sustainable.

Done properly, offshore outsourcing can be one of the most powerful tools available to small businesses to improve their business and financial results.   Done incorrectly, it can cause significant operational problems and financial damage.   Success depends predominantly on the ability of businesses to make informed choices about the location, service provider and activities to be offshored and make offshoring a long term, strategic commitment.

Appendix

City Comparison – Key Indian Outsourcing Centres

Mumbai	
Manpower:	169,000 college / university graduates per year
Telecom Infrastructure:	16 - 18 prominent Internet service providers, with nine telecom service providers
Emerging Trends (Verticals):	Financial Research, Back office research
Real Estate (Average rent U.S.$ / Sq Ft / Month):	0.73 - 0.75
Major companies situated in Mumbai:	JP Morgan, Transworks, Infowavz, Efunds, Rolta India, Tata Consultancy, Standard Chartered, HSBC, American Express, Delphi Corporation, Prudential
Chennai	
Manpower:	100,000 college / university graduates per year
Telecom Infrastructure:	14 - 16 prominent Internet service providers, with five telecom service providers
Emerging Trends (Verticals):	R&D, Medical Transcription, Back Office, Financial Processing, CAD/CAM and is slowly emerging in Software development
Real Estate (Average rents U.S.$ / Sq Ft / Month):	0.712 - 0.78
Major companies situated in Chennai:	Verizon, EDS, Hexaware, Sutherland Technologies, HP, eGlobal, Ford Motors, The World Bank, AIG, Qwest Communications

Pune	
Manpower:	100,000 college / university graduates per year
Telecom Infrastructure:	14 - 16 prominent Internet service providers, with six telecom service providers
Emerging Trends (Verticals):	CAD, CAM automotive, software development
Real Estate (Average rents U.S.$ / Sq Ft / Month):	0.62 - 0.67
Major companies situated in Chennai:	Msource, Spectramind, WNS, Wipro, Infosys, Cognizant Technology Solutions, Mahindra British Telecom, IBM, HSBC
New Delhi	
Manpower:	295,000 college / university graduates per year
Telecom Infrastructure:	14 - 16 prominent Internet service providers, with six telecom service providers
Emerging Trends (Verticals):	Low end back office processing & voice based
Real Estate (Average rents U.S.$ / Sq Ft / Month):	0.623 - 0.712 (Gurgaon) 0.23 - 0.27 (Noida)
Major companies situated in Delhi:	Hughes Software Systems, American Express, Sapient, Hewlett Packard, Xansa, Keane Systems, EXL Services, Computer Science Corporation, Adobe Systems, General Electric Co.
Hyderabad	
Manpower:	80,000 college / university graduates per year
Telecom Infrastructure:	14 - 16 prominent Internet

	service providers, with two telecom service providers
Emerging Trends (Verticals):	Software, Back office, product design
Real Estate (Average rents U.S.$ / Sq Ft / Month):	0.82 – 0.86
Major companies situated in Hyderabad:	Dell, Microsoft, Infosys, Virtusa, Oracle, GE Capital, ADP Wilco, Delloite Consulting, Eastman Chemical Co, HSBC
Kolkata	
Manpower:	300,000 college / university graduates per year
Telecom Infrastructure:	14 - 16 prominent Internet service providers, with six telecom service providers
Emerging Trends (Verticals):	Consulting and Software
Real Estate (Average rents U.S.$ / Sq Ft / Month):	0.72 – 0.75
Major companies situated in Chennai:	IBM, The Chatterjee Group, TCS, Wipro, Satyam

[Source: NASSCOM: "There is more to India than Bangalore"- January / February 2005
http://www.nasscom.org/bponewsline/jan05/RealEstateCorner.asp]

Useful Web Links

Accenture – Research & Insights
(http://www.accenture.com/xd/xd.asp?it=enweb&xd=ideas\ideas_home.xml)

BPO India (http://www.bpoindia.org/research/)

CFO (http://www.cfo.com/)

CIO (http://www.cio.com/)

E-business Strategies (http://www.ebstrategy.com/BPO/Default.htm)

The Economist (http://www.economist.com/)

Forrester (http://www.forrester.com/findresearch)

McKinsey Quarterly (http://www.mckinsey.com/ideas/mck_quarterly/)

National Association of Software and Service Companies
(http://www.nasscom.org/)

National Outsourcing Association (http://www.noa.co.uk/)

Offshoring Digest (http://www.offshoring-digest.com/)

Offshore Outsourcing World (http://www.enterblog.com/index.html)

Outsourcing – The Global Service Directory (http://www.outsourcing.org/)

Outsourcing Centre (http://www.outsourcing-offshore.com/)

The Outsourcing Institute (http://www.outsourcing.com/index.html)

Oxford BPO Research (http://www.bporesearch.com/)

References

Accenture / The Economist Intelligence Unit (Jun 2004) *Outsourcing the Finance Function: Achieving High Performance in Governance and Control*

Agrawal V, et. al. (2003) *Offshoring and Beyond.* The McKinsey Quarterly

Alvarez E, et. al. (Aug 2003) *Making Overhead Outperform : Next-Generation G&A Performance.* Euromoney / Booz Allen Hamilton

Corporate Executive Board (Jan 2004) *Outsourcing in the Financial Services Sector.* Washington

Corporate Executive Board (Apr 2004) *The Current State of Business Process Offshoring.* Washington

Craig D and Willmott P (Feb 2005) *Outsourcing Grows Up.* The McKinsey Quarterly

De Filippo G, et. al. (2005) *Can China Compete in IT Services ?* The McKinsey Quarterly

DiamondCluster (2005) *2005 Global IT Outsourcing Report*

DTi Small Business Service (2003) *Annual Small Business Survey 2003*

Farrell D, et. al.(2005) *Sizing the Emerging Global Labor Market.* The McKinsey Quarterly

Greiner, L (Jul / Aug 1972) *Evolution and Revolution as Organisations Grow.* Harvard Business Review

Hatch, P J (Oct 2004) *Offshore 2005 Research - Preliminary Findings and Conclusions.* Ventoro

ITAA (Mar 2004) *The Impact of Offshore IT Software and Services Outsourcing on the U.S. Economy and the IT Industry.* Global Insight (U.S.A) Inc.

M2 Presswire (Feb 2005) *Competition Intensifies for Global Offshoring.* M2 Communications

McKinsey Global Institute (Aug 2003) *Offshoring: Is it a Win-Win Game ?.* McKinsey Company

McKinsey Global Institute (Oct 2003) *Preface to the Information Technology / Business Process Offshoring Case.* McKinsey Global Institute

McKinsey Global Institute (Oct 2003) *New Horizons: Multinational Company Investment in Developing Economies*

Miller N and Stone K (Jul 2004) *Offshore Outsourcing - safeguarding personal data.* The Lawyer Group

Moloney K (May 2005) *In Practice Employment - Tomorrow's People.* Accountancy

O'Connor B (Nov 2004) *Confederation of British Industry supports retraining - and offshoring.* London: Daily Mail

Odindo C, Diacon, S, Ennew C (2004) *Outsourcing in the U.K. Financial Services Industry: The Asian Offshore Market.* Nottingham University Business School

Scott M and Bruce R (Jun 1987) *Five Stages of Growth in Small Business.* Pergamon Journals

Sunday Herald (Nov 2003) *If the rich nations really wanted these jobs why didn't they value them ?* Sunday Herald

Valanju S (Jul /Aug 2005) *Site Unseen?* Financial Management

Index

Kolkata · 71, 89

overheads · 7, 25, 39

www.ingramcontent.com/pod-product-compliance
Lightning Source LLC
Chambersburg PA
CBHW031951190326
41519CB00007B/751